PLAYING DOCTOR; PART THREE: CHIEF RESIDENT

(FUMBLING TOWARDS MEDICAL PRACTICE)

JOHN LAWRENCE

eBook ISBN: 978-1-7355072-6-2

Paperback ISBN: 978-1-7355072-5-5

Edited by Anne Cole Norman

Cover Design by Caroline Johnson

❀ Created with Vellum

For Chandler, Nico, Mattias & Luca

CONTENTS

PREFACE

This third, and possibly final, book in the series represents the culminating arc from a head-injured medical student into a licensed and practicing physician. Not that receiving a license and finishing residency represents the end of your medical education by any means. But at that moment, pushed from the ivory tower of formal medical training, you are expected to start happily working as a doctor. Much to my advisors (and friends and parents) frustration however, I continually questioned my decision about becoming a doctor.

Those uncertainties were partially generated from fears that I could never fulfill the role of a good doctor (imposter syndrome). At the same time I had very authentic concerns that I was only tromping down this medical path because I lacked the courage to pursue my dreams of writing and filmmaking—career paths not so completely judged by a system of meritocracy like medicine where the hoops to jump through are more clearly laid out to succeed— or at least attain your degree.

Regardless of my continuous internal monologues interrogating the purpose of my life and debating whether I disliked medicine for the amount of note-writing and dictation, the hours in the hospital, or because I felt the self-imposed, student-debt burdened life was selfishly keeping me from doing what I really wanted (talk about self-sabotage), I still wanted to give patients the best care possible. Not the most noble of motivating factors, but guilt and fear of not treating patients appropriately drove me to work hard throughout my training and years in practice.

I hope you enjoy this book about the final year of residency training—perhaps more medically oriented than the first two in the series-- and my initial forays into medical practice, where I embark on a new, practical learning curve that would continue to climb over all my subsequent years in healthcare. So, perhaps a fourth book remains to be written.

Meanwhile, please recognize that the tone in the book is often flippant and intended to be tongue-in-cheek. While my self-mockery should be evident, I have the utmost respect for the profession and the people involved. My own frustrations at not attaining the high bar set by the doctors around me is usually the reason for my occasional rants as I seek to place blame anywhere but on myself. Please know this is all for entertainment, not medical advice, nor deep commentary on medical training. I feel incredibly fortunate to have trained where I did and with so many dedicated teachers—the respect did not always go both ways, but that was my fault.

INTRODUCTION

BREATHING LIFE INTO UPHOLSTERY

Perhaps it was an attempt to garner attention. We'll never know. But right in the middle of a somewhat pretentious cocktail party, an apparently over-served guest suddenly collapsed. While this sprawling act of unconsciousness certainly added spice to the otherwise dull event, my amusement was brief. All eyes in the hushed room, now turned to me, the doctor in the background sipping his cocktail.

Under all that uninvited social pressure, I felt obliged to put down my drink and do something to help the party casualty. I walked over, knelt by the victim and felt for a pulse—which was either non-existent or playing extremely hard to find.

Ok, think...No pulse... need to start CPR.

Crap. Since graduating from residency training only three months ago, I hadn't performed CPR on a single person. Not even for fun.

Alright, just like riding a bike, I thought to myself. An analogy I had proven to be mildly ridiculous over the last years with a few too many bike accidents landing me on the wrong side of the doctor/patient relationship. At this point however, I did not think I could make matters much worse.

I took a deep breath and started administering chest compressions, feeling the scrutinizing eyes of my audience boring into my technique. As if I needed to feel even more tension in this already stressful situation.

It had taken me eight long and circuitous years, along with a mountain of financial debt to be right here, reviving a lifeless body.

I stopped the compressions, felt for a pulse, and listened for any sounds of spontaneous breathing.

Nothing.

I looked around the room with mild despair, my facial expressions striving to convey appropriate shock that my efforts were futile. This was not going to be a lifesaving day, totally marring my heroic gesture. Apparently just like falling off a bike would have been a more apropos statement.

I stoically announced to the rather unimpressed crowd, "There's no pulse. We've lost him."

It was the first patient I had lost since graduating from residency, the first patient to die under my care since becoming a fully trained physician.

Fortunately the victim was a lounge chair cushion.

Literally.

Unfortunately for me, the not so captivated onlookers were several Hollywood producers and a director.

I had been auditioning for a new SHOWTIME channel television pilot called, *PARADISE*; and after that far from brilliant performance, I would *not* be playing the nameless "DOCTOR" in the pilot's cocktail party scene.

Yes, I jumped ahead of myself to give you a taste of the exciting actor-doctor life waiting for me after graduating residency training. One advantage of the job I eventually took in urgent care was only working several long shifts each week. The rest of my days were free to enjoy writing and auditioning for acting roles. And for some reason my agent sent me to audition for every "doctor" role that came to town.

It's not that sending me out to audition for roles as a doctor was completely farfetched since I was acting as one in real life, but every time I went to an audition I was told, "You don't look like a doctor." When casting-agents and producers think of doctors, they imagine grey-haired, Norman Rockwell painting type gentlemen, not a young fellow that looks like he's taking pre-med classes to improve his flailing social life. But ironically here I was, a real-life doctor, unable to land a role playing one on TV.

So after that failed audition, the actor in me, unable to accept that I was wrong for the role of a doctor, critiqued my performance.

My chest compression technique had been good, nice position, proper timing. Perhaps I had put too much emphasis on conveying my dismay? Or maybe my line delivery was off? I had delivered the line, *"There's no pulse. We've lost him,"* with a serious soap opera tone, portraying my defeat at not reviving the furniture.

But come on, the words, "There's no pulse, we've lost him," sounded a bit silly. I likely stunted what minuscule amounts of natural acting flair I possessed with concern that I might sub-consciously change the line to, "Oh no, we've lost the cushion!" And honestly, who says, "There's no pulse, we've lost him," anyway? First of all, there could always be some unexpected flip-pant act of God, so there was no reason to get all uppity and dramatic about not having a pulse.

Secondly, in the contemporary, cover your ass, legal-medical environment, it never looked good to be the one admitting to losing anything, especially people, it appeared irresponsible, even at a fictional cocktail party.

What I should have done was throw the line away, like losing a pulse didn't matter, and muttered something under my breath about having misplaced my cocktail, "There's no pulse. *(sotto voce)* *Just like this party.* Hey! Who stole my gin and tonic?"

The resulting lack of a role on the doomed pilot would have been the same, but at least I would have made a more daring choice. Although, to credit my acting classes, I did eventually get to play a doctor on TV—which fortunately had nothing to do with my inability to revive upholstery.

The above story, as mentioned, took place after I *spoiler alert* graduated from residency training. I know it's not chronological, but I wanted to share an introductory story that sparked your interest because compared to the mildly traumatic openings of *Playing Doctor,* parts one and two, there was nothing remarkable about the start of my senior year of residency training.

Medical school (book one) opened right after I suffered several bike-crash-induced head injuries that resulted in a bleed in my brain, amnesia, and a massive case of imposter syndrome to start medical school. The start of residency (book two) opened with me missing a potentially fatal diagnosis in one of my closest friends— a colossal blunder confirming that my imposter syndrome was real and appropriate, and making me doubt my limited abilities as a physician all the more.

Fair enough, I missed Scott's collapsed lung, but we were biking 100 miles a day together and apart from the pesky complaint about his chest hurting, he seemed fine. Good news, he's alive and still riding all these years later. So, all ended well... except it's not the end, I still had a final year of training.

So now here we are at the start of book three, my senior year, my final year of training, and apart from the residency program keeping me on top secret probation, my life was relatively calm and normal. Over the next twelve months I would continue working on clinical rotations as well as serving as the chief resident overseeing the junior residents in the hospital. And the year started without any harrowing events, which after the previous books more notable opening moments, seemed rather dull and commonplace. Maybe I was maturing? Maybe I was making better life choices? And maybe the sun was rising in the West, I don't know, but even my usually comical personal life was free of drama. I had actually just met a lovely woman, and very soon we would start dating—but give me a month or two, I can screw things up relatively quickly.

So with everything starting off way too smoothly, I gave you that failed CPR adventure to open the book and tease your appetite for more upcoming medical misadventures. Because, to attain that summit of medical competence, self-assuredly commanding the unsuccessful resuscitation of a cocktail party pillow, required that I first attempt and fail at running some real medical code situations (we learn from our errors, not our successes)—which foreshadows that I was going to crash, burn, flag and flail a whole lot in the next twelve months if I was to learn enough to graduate and be out on my own in medical practice. I was not feeling competent enough to be practicing medicine on my own. But the senior resident role was the perfect place to high-light firsthand what you did, and more often for me, did not know about practicing medicine and running hospital teams.

DURING THAT FINAL YEAR, ALL OF US SENIOR RESIDENTS WOULD share time as the Chief Resident, leading the family practice resident teams. Having been under various senior resident's rule over the last years, some benign and others tyrannical, I had thoughts and opinions on how to wield the chief's power (But more on that later).

Our three years as family practice residents almost followed the lines of the medical training adage: *see one, do one, teach one.* During the first year we were overwhelmed with grunt labor-- mostly *seeing* real doctors as we scurried about writing notes and taking care of scut work. By the second year, you were *doing* the work. And then in our third year, along with completing the rest of your clinical rotation training, your role included *teaching* the junior residents during your months as chief resident.

I had questioned completing my residency training throughout the previous years, but now, only twelve months from graduation, I relaxed into the idea of completing the whole thing. I still wanted to make films and started attending weekly acting classes as much as my call schedule allowed. I was still coaching the junior ski racing team in the winter. I was still training for marathons. I still had Winston, the horribly mischievous Labrador. I felt pretty good moving into this third year.

I even felt relaxed about taking on the responsibilities of chief resident. We senior residents had experienced working with various chiefs over the last years and mostly knew what was required. So I felt ready to step into the role. Of course, less than 24 hours after crossing the Rubicon from second year resident to instantly being a senior/chief resident, I would fall flat on my face in a code situation with slightly higher stakes than my furniture resuscitating audition. Fortunately, I would also get many shots at redemption. So, let's jump right into the final year of residency training and prepare to fail, big time.

THE MOLE

CODES GONE WILD

My first day as a senior resident was rather nice. I had the day off.

Our residency schedule was still structured around hospital and clinical rotations, but now included several required months serving as the "Chief Resident." As family practice chief resident your responsibilities included being in charge of the hospital residents and all the patients under their care, overseeing the admittance of patients to our service from the ER or doctor's offices, taking care of the patients in hospital, and teaching at rounds.

The chief was present in the hospital during the day from 8 a.m. until 6 p.m., but at night, since hospital patients weren't sent home for dinner, and more of them usually showed up to be admitted overnight, we had a position called "The Mole." And just as the nocturnal name suggests, the mole worked as the nighttime chief resident.

I started my senior year as the mole. Hence, the reason for having the *day* off.

So, on that first day of my third year I enjoyed a long bike ride, ate lunch at home, and then twiddled my thumbs all the way until 6 p.m. Retrospectively, it might have behooved me to spend a few minutes reviewing inpatient adult hospital medicine, but I figured that there would be plenty of time for such studious affairs once the mole gig was underway. An assumption I made that was complete bunk.

The overnight shift, 6 p.m. until 8 a.m. the next morning, was only fourteen-hours—not so bad when we were used to 36-hour stints. But the mole also worked a full shift over the weekend (from 8 a.m. to 8 a.m. the next day), and you were expected to see patients in your clinic. So being the mole, despite having some free hours of daylight, could add up to a 120-hour workweek.

During weekdays, the chief had attending physicians present in the hospital to add some backup. And typically, for the most part, the junior residents we oversaw only required mild supervision such as checking on their written orders and helping direct their thinking as we admitted and evaluated patients. They could normally be trusted to alert us to any patient concerns. A normal in-patient medical team usually included a mix of first- and second-year residents, so there was a good balance of experience.

Except right now it was July. And July is when medical residents start their first rotation. The new interns had been doctors for one full day—just as their supposed overnight leader (that's me) had been mole for, well, almost a full minute. And now at nighttime, the attending physicians were not in the hospital (that's why the residents were there, so attending physicians could be home in bed).

That first evening, I headed into the hospital relaxed and confident, ready to demonstrate that I'd learned enough to work as a real doctor. I was prepared with a good attitude and my years of training to help care for the team's sick patients.

Truth be told (and this would come back to bite me in several hours), I had not taken care of any sick adults in a hospital setting for several months. My last months of clinical rotations had consisted of 1) caring for pregnant women on the labor and delivery deck, 2) evaluating newborns in the nursery, and 3) treating injured kids in the pediatric ER. It's fair to say in hindsight that I might have benefitted from a smattering of review before taking charge of the entire adult hospital service. But I was confident (which typically leads to me making a mistake) that my strolling back through those incandescently lit hallways would instantly stimulate adult medicine knowledge to re-spark the appropriate synapses of my brain.

Enough drama. I showed up with my positive attitude and greeted the daytime chief I was relieving. After one day in charge, she looked absolutely haggard and sounded even grumpier. Apparently the chief role was a bit grueling, which did not bode well for me. She checked out all the team's patients to me in a booklet of large blue index cards. Each card had the relevant medical information for a patient we were in charge of keeping alive in the hospital. This stack of blue cards was sort of the baton, conch shell, or crown passed to whomever was in charge of the resident team, and for the first time ever, the cards were in my clutches; I was officially in command.

This daytime chief resident was typically a very cheery and friendly woman. She curtly reviewed the patient cards with me, then hurried towards the exit door, mentioning that there were a few sick patients in the ICU she hoped I would have time to check on. And then she left without even wishing me good luck. I started to wonder if she would show up to relieve me the next morning—given her dour demeanor, her return was a bit uncertain.

As for visiting the sick people in the ICU, I trusted that they were in good hands already. The weeks could potentially pass by without me ever seeing some of the patients on the service if they remained relatively stable overnight, and therefore not requiring my attention. Alternatively, one sick patient who became sicker and turned unstable (such as having breathing problems) could require you spend your entire night bedside monitoring changes. If several patients became unstable and several more were admitted, you had a long night to survive.

Really diligent moles started their evening by stopping by every patient's room, reading over their charts and making sure there was nothing more we could be doing for their care that had not already been thought of during the daytime—a fresh set of eyes to review and think through complicated cases. I knew I didn't have anything brilliant to add to what the attending doctors already had working; therefore, in everyone's best interest, I did my part by not poking around where I was not needed. And I did really hope that nobody got any sicker or died. At least not while I was in the hospital.

That first night started off with several routine patient admissions from the ER onto the hospital floors. We admitted one patient with pneumonia and another with pancreatitis. No problem. My role, supervising the residents on the team, meant that the most tedious aspects of hospital admissions, writing long notes and orders, were carried out by the residents, thereby granting me more time to concentrate on the actual patient care and teaching. We were just busy enough that any hopes of dinner were a pipedream.

As the interns wrote admission notes describing the patient's illness, physical exam and medical conditions, we discussed appropriate admission orders, such as which medications to start, what labs or radiological studies to order, and then the patients were taken to their rooms.

Suddenly, discussing cases with the second-year resident on call that night, and advising him on standard treatment protocols, made it surprisingly apparent that I might actually know what I was doing.

This new awareness was a mild revelation and for those initial hours, as I oversaw and taught the admitting resident, I began to feel falsely confident that I was becoming a decent doctor.

The feeling was appropriately brief. At midnight I was paged to admit our third patient from the ER.

Strolling the dark, peaceful hallways towards the ER, anticipating another good learning case where I could share some teaching points with the junior resident, I heard the overhead PA voice announce, *"CODE BLUE ICU. CODE BLUE ICU."*

Codes were usually enjoyable—perhaps not for the patients—but mildly so for the code team staff. It was hands-on, active work, fighting to save a life. In the middle of the night, with few doctors in the hospital, I knew I would get to be more involved than usual in this code. I raced down several hallways, screeching around blind hospital corners before bursting through the ICU doors, and sliding into the patient's room, slightly breathless, but ready to help as needed.

The first thing I noticed was a very sick appearing, elderly patient lying in the ICU bed staring at me.

Recall now that my previous several months of residency training consisted of working in:

1) The Pediatric Emergency Room.

2) The Newborn Nursery.

3) The Labor and Delivery Deck (Obstetrics).

And most recently:

4) Admitting two very routine patients earlier this same evening.

So at this precise moment, any patient not pediatric, pregnant, or routine was a bit of a medical mystery to me. But even in my underprepared state, I could see that something was seriously wrong with this patient. He somehow, magically, managed to appear paler than the white hospital sheets covering him—possibly a reflection of poor lighting, or perhaps inadequate hospital sheet laundering—either way he was impressively pale.

I then noticed a cardiac monitor displaying some chaotic,

alien-like, heart rhythm that I stood no chance of interpreting. It was absolutely bizarre and bore slim resemblance to any human or other animal heart tracings I had ever seen.

Finally I noticed someone else entering the room. A nurse. Oh good, we could start taking care of the patient.

But the nurse just stood staring at me.

Why is she staring at me? She should be helping the patient.

Aha. I realized that she was waiting for someone to give her orders.

And then it dawned on me...very slowly...

By some freak astral misalignment, or the flub of my having faster shoes than anyone else in the hospital (damn marathon training), I had arrived at the code before a single other person.

Oh, shit.

For some ungodly reason there were no other doctors in the room. No ICU doctors. No ER doctors. No television doctors. No other doctors, nurses, or ER staff coming to rescue the patient. There was just me and one nurse. Usually the room would be packed with medically astute people by now—but it wasn't.

So, the nurse stood looking at me, the resident-mole-doctor, waiting for orders to start doing something.

What the hell, besides blatantly ignoring a code alarm, was everybody else doing? Their selfish and irresponsible disregard for patient care left me, the chief resident of almost four hours, in charge of the goddamn code.

And I ran that notion through my overloaded synapses one more time... I was in charge of the code. I was the doctor in the room charged with saving this dying patient's life.

You are likely salivating, realizing that I was in the midst of a medical resident's wet dream, being granted the opportunity to single handedly save a life in a code situation. The years of medical training under my scrub-ties were about to be on heroic, heart-warming display.

And I had no idea what to do.

I looked down at the expiring patient, glanced at the bizarre tracing on his EKG, and instead of thinking of anything worthwhile, my mind went blank. I'm talking completely blank, as in parts of my brain stopped functioning, and the use of my tongue and the entire English language failed me completely.

Why, oh why, couldn't it be a straightforward MI? *An MI! My stethoscope for an MI!* (MI stands for Myocardial Infarction, i.e. a heart attack, something I could handle three-quarters asleep while cooking omelets).

I must have been breathing, but otherwise I was paralyzed, unable to put any rational thoughts together, let alone verbalize them.

Several paltry reflections drifted through the windswept desert of my cranium: I revisited the fact that I had not done any adult medicine in six months. I had forgotten my code cards in the call room—the code cards which listed the medical protocols I could follow in this situation. I was also due to re-certify my ACLS training in two weeks—which is where they would re-instruct me what to do in this exact situation.

My mouth was really dry. I could not speak. I stared like a mute deer into the headlights of this dying patient's eyes and heard a distant sea breeze between my ears louder than the names of any medicines that might be useful. I could not think of the name of a single medicine on a grocery or pharmacy shelf.

The entire practice of medicine had completely deserted me.

My blank stare was not instilling confidence in anybody, myself included. I needed to do something, anything.

But what?

My usual medical treatment options in the last months of pediatric and obstetric care included sedating children in order to repair lacerations, delivering pregnant mothers' infants, or calculating the gross intake of formula in the nursery. None of these seemed viable options—although, to be fair to the patient, I did consider them.

Fortunately more people started trickling into the room. Unfortunately, not a single one of them was the least bit helpful. My junior resident finally appeared, and imagine this, rather than trying to impress me with his keen knowledge of code situations, he too stared at me, waiting for orders.

More nurses magically filled the room, and they just stared at me as well.

The patient gaped at me—no doubt preparing to use his last breath to exhort me into some form of action.

Realizing I had to do something as the room's complete and suffocating inertia was becoming embarrassing, I considered my alternatives:

1) Turn and run out of the room.

2) Feign a stroke.

3) Vomit.

These were the best solutions I could come up with at short notice. I chose door number one, turned to run—but standing right there behind me was the Emergency Room doctor for the night.

Thank God. Certainly he'd know what to do since I could not make heads or tails of the EKG tracing. We could finally save this patient, go admit the other patient waiting in the ER, and all get some sleep.

Now prepare to be shocked; instead of saving the patient, the ER doctor turned to me and said, "Well, you're in charge, better do something."

I had worked with this particular doctor on many occasions, and he knew I was normally quite competent. So in some sort of sensei teaching moment, he now waited to see how I would handle this stressful moment…

How did I handle it? Well, we stood there, immobilized, for what felt like several more hours, waiting for my speech to return. So I think the correct answer to '*How did I handle the stressful moment?*' is not very well at all.

Finally the ER doctor whispered, "Maybe some Lidocaine?"

I nodded my head, still unable to figure out what to do or say. I heard another whisper from the doctor, "There's an algorithm in your pocketbook."

We carried certain books with us (yes, this is pre-smart phone era), one being a small pharmacopoeia of all the medicines we ordered and their dosages. Also included in the book were protocols for treating coding patients, like this one with a heart arrhythmia in front of me. The book would tell me what dosage of Lidocaine to order for this patient with an alien heart rhythm.

I took the book from my scrub pocket and turned to the back pages. In the hazy distance, a slur of words, spoken in a voice that sounded vaguely similar to mine, ordered Lidocaine, ordered labs, and suddenly the time-space continuum returned to normal, and everybody went into action.

For all I know I had only blanked out on what to do or say for several seconds, or maybe it was several hours—regardless, it sucked and felt absolutely humiliating.

That was one of the single worst moments I experienced as a resident—completely unprepared for a code situation. It was my responsibility to have been prepared and to have reviewed adult code protocols for that exact situation.

Instead, I made sure my infantile defense mechanisms were still functioning (they were), and I decided it was really unfair to expect me to be ready for a difficult case on my first night as the mole in charge of anything—especially after several months working on clinical services unrelated to this inpatient adult medicine buffoonery.

No, it wasn't really unfair. It was precisely my responsibility to handle that situation and run codes.

When we finally admitted the patient who had been waiting in the ER, I mindlessly provided the resident with some teaching points. But I could not focus well because my thoughts were consumed with the knowledge that if the coding patient had died, it would have been my fault. A legal team would look at the notes and see that the chief resident had stood mutely in the room with no idea what to do. Then I would appear on the front of the local newspaper, rightfully charged with being inept and a miscreant.

The next morning I went home and dutifully pored over every codebook, ACLS manual, cookbook, and boy scout first aid pamphlet, making sure every single resident under my supervision would be ready for any and every future code situation.

SEVERAL DAYS LATER MY CODE STUDIES WERE REWARDED.

"CODE BLUE ICU. CODE BLUE ICU."

I raced through the halls to the ICU ready for vindication, ready to take charge, ready to run whatever possible code situation awaited me. I would run this code perfectly. Redemption was at hand!

I barged into the ICU and headed towards the coding patient's room prepared to singlehandedly save the day. But the patient's doorway was blocked by the entire population of the hospital fighting to get into the room. I couldn't even see into the room over the wall of doctors, nurses, medical students, and residents cramming to work the code before me.

But I refused to be thwarted. I needed to prove to everyone present that my previous ICU code debacle had been a fluke.

Since I was the chief resident, I elbowed into the packed and sweltering room and politely relieved the attending physician (who was getting tired) from doing chest compressions. I started rhythmically compressing the unconscious patient's chest and asked, "What happened?"

Simple answer: a medical procedure had put the patient's heart into a fatal heart rhythm.

If you're a stickler for medical details, read on for the complete answer (if not, feel free to skip ahead a few pages).

Have you ever heard a doctor say something like, "This is a very safe treatment, there's a one in a thousand chance of anything going wrong"? It sounds like a very routine and safe treatment, right?

Unless you're the one.

This person happened to be the one.

Days earlier, this now unconscious patient had developed an abnormal heart rhythm called atrial-fibrillation (A-fib). People are actually able to live with A-fib just fine. But there are possible complications from A-fib, so, it's preferable to treat those patients and get their heart back into a normal rhythm.

Quick A-fib lesson: The healthy heart is an elegant pumping system that is perfectly coordinated by electrical signals. Normally, the upper chambers of the heart (atriums) fill with blood, then pump that blood into the lower chambers of the heart (ventricles). The ventricles then pump blood into your lungs and body.

But in A-fib, the atriums march to the beat of their own drummer—more like a toddler wildly banging pots and pans than a skilled drummer—and atriums contracting in a rowdy manner are unable to properly fill up, or pump out, blood. Your normally well-conducted Swiss ticking machine becomes inefficient, pumping less blood into the body, thereby causing blood pressure to drop, which makes people feel lousy.

And if feeling crummy wasn't bad enough, blood not pumped out of the atriums, just sitting there, can turn into a blood clot. If that clot then dislodges, it will leave the atrium, travel through the blood vessels, and get stuck in the person's lungs, heart, or brain—causing worse situations than feeling lousy.

In order to avoid the potential pulmonary embolus, stroke, or heart attack scenario respectively, patients with A-fib were typically started on medication to prevent blood clots from forming.

Patients who had been in A-fib less than a few days, however, would not have had time to develop a blood clot and could safely be "cardioverted" back into a normal heart rhythm without starting them on blood thinners.

Cardioversion, i.e. converting someone back (from A-fib in this case) to their normal and safe heart rhythm, was accomplished in two acceptable manners. The first used medications to put the heart back into sinus (normal) rhythm. The second involved using an electrical shock, like what you see if someone was being shocked back to life after their heart stopped.

A third method was always mentioned, the "chest thump." The chest thump was exactly what it sounded like—you thumped the patient, hard, across their chest with your arm. No one verified if it worked well and it was definitely not acceptable in the ICU to just slam your arm down across a patient's chest, *but* it's worth trying if you're out in the wilderness one day and your friend pipes up, "Uh-oh, my A-fib is getting worse, and my blood pressure is dropping." If they suddenly fall to the forest floor unconscious, go ahead and deliver a good chest thump.

One of the craziest patient stories I ever encountered involved a man who had been struck by lightning while rock climbing. The electrical blast had stopped his heart and he fell around 15-meters onto rocks. Now, slamming onto rocks at high velocity was a rather extreme version of the chest thump, but it had worked. The patient's heart re-started. Granted, there were a few other complications from that very exciting, electrical dismount with traumatic thump, of a crash landing—but the patient survived.

Long tangent over, let's jump back to the ICU code. This patient with A-fib had experienced some mild fatigue from low blood pressure but had otherwise been doing fine. He had been able to walk, talk, and keep blood flowing into important organs, like his kidneys and brain. Note the use of the words *"had been."*

The medical team then chose to electrically Zap the patient to correct his heart rhythm.

A senior resident had convinced both the patient and cardiologist that electro-cardioversion should be used to convert the heart of this gelatinous 300-pound gentleman back into normal rhythm given that no blood clot would have had time to form yet.

The resident was so certain of success that he even bet the cardiologist a bottle of wine that the procedure would work. Now, the cardiologist must have been pretty certain it was a good idea too for him to actually proceed with this normally safe procedure —but all procedures had risks.

When the patient was shocked, his heart went into ventricular fibrillation (V-fib). Fibbing in general is not considered polite, and V-fib is worse than A-fib. V-fib means the ventricles responsible for pumping blood through the body were beating so fast and so chaotically, that they couldn't even fill with blood, i.e. the ventricles frenzied contractions were not pumping blood through the body.

The resulting lack of oxygen to the patient's brain, heart and other vital organs was the reason he was unconscious and I was now missing Sunday brunch.

Various thoughts entered my mind at this point, including: The optimistic, *Well this will make the day pass quicker.*

The self-centered realist: *This guy's going to die soon anyway, I wonder if there will be any bagels left when the code is done?*

And most importantly, the newly confident authoritarian figure on codes that now spat out different medicine options and then asked: "Want me to start a central line?" I'm not sure if any of my opinions were listened to, but as nothing else seemed to be working, I threw out comments, advice, and protocols, one after another. After refreshing my code protocols all week, I was now, in my mind, the most up-to-date expert in the room.

By the time we were finished doing CPR, starting central lines, administering boatloads of expensive medicines and shocking the patient repeatedly, he was still alive. We had prolonged the patient's existence in that hospital bed for at least a few more hours.

We had successfully taken a guy who had been mildly sick that morning, albeit eating and talking, and managed to leave him intubated (on a respirator) with kidney failure. As mentioned, plenty of people just live with A-fib and take pills to avoid any major issues. Tough case to reflect on as I was only involved with the code. But there is a balance in medicine, a field where the healthcare team feels it is their responsibility to make people better—but sometimes bad things happen when we do typically safe procedures. Medicine in general aims to be conservative in its treatments for good reason. And the treatment in this case was the correct one—it just did not go well. Sadly, the patient died from one of the above complications later that week.

I don't think anyone collected the bottle of wine.

BEING CHIEF MOLE ALSO MEANT BEING RESPONSIBLE FOR ALL THE other residents and their patients on different services, such as obstetrics. Over the years, the nurses on the labor and delivery deck had learned to trust my obstetric abilities and would often call me in for tough cases they did not want treated by an unprepared intern, or for emergency deliveries. One such night they paged me overhead to hurry to the labor and delivery deck as a woman was imminently delivering. The nurses weren't fond of the resident on call that evening and hadn't had time to call an attending. As I've always stated, be nice to the nurses, respect them, they are there to help the patients and you—in that order. You do not want disrespected nurses ignoring you as was happening to the other resident in this case.

I ran down the hall and into the delivery room where a nurse was hurriedly setting up the tray with everything we used for deliveries. I was in the middle of placing a glove on one hand when the baby's head suddenly appeared between the patient's legs.

Hello!

Much as we all looked forward to greeting this young fellow, I wanted to slow down his arrival to prevent his mother from having an explosive delivery and potential ugly vaginal laceration. And I'm not sure how welcome the baby would have felt if he delivered himself by launching from between his mother's legs, flying through the air, and crashing onto a cold tile floor. At the same time, I didn't really want blood on my hands from a patient I did not know—not that it was a social foible to be bloodied before proper introductions, but rather, I had no idea if this patient had any blood-borne diseases I should be concerned about contacting.

So, I placed my one, semi-gloved hand on the baby's head and held out my other hand, calling, "I need a glove. Can someone get me a glove? A glove? *My kingdom for a glove?*" But receiving a second glove was not going to happen, as the nurse was still opening the delivery tray which contained the umbilical cord clamps and bulb suction. And the baby arrived in my hands without anyone applauding my Shakespearean reference.

Amidst the confusion, I made sure everything was OK with the baby's breathing, which it was, and then decided to cut the cord. The umbilical cord has blood in it and is under pressure, so when you cut the cord there is often a spurt of blood that you normally shield with your hand. But I did not want to shield the cord with my ungloved hand, so when the cord was cut, blood shot from the umbilical cord and spray-painted the yellow sweater of the new grandmother who, seconds before, had been standing right next to me.

Once more, please note my use of the words *had been.*

Upon seeing the blood splattered across her sweater, the grandmother promptly fainted and collapsed backwards onto the floor. I only had two hands to catch patients and mine were currently occupied. Fortunately nothing serious happened to the grandmother.

HOURS LATER, AS THE SUN ROSE, I WAS BACK IN THE ER HAVING A rousing discussion with a woman who, despite being admitted to the hospital after suffering a mild stroke, was described to me as remaining mentally sharp as a tack. She had fallen in the middle of the night, and we were admitting her for some testing.

I state that the conversation was rousing because we were all over the map. The resident kept trying to focus the conversation on the patient's medical history and what had caused the patient to fall. The patient, however, wanted to know when she could go home, despite being told repeatedly we wanted her to stay in the hospital.

Meanwhile, I kept bringing the conversation back to my recent discovery that this 86-year-old woman, who admitted to having some vision problems—as in, she couldn't see directly in front of herself due to macular degeneration—still drove her automobile on real roads.

The part of the tale I found most harrowing to my own tenuous existence was that she lived at the top of a canyon where my friends and I frequently bicycled.

"How long will I be here?" she asked yet again.

"Hold on, let's go back. You actually have a driver's license?" I asked incredulously.

"Oh yes, can I drive home now?" she asked, concerned with why we were keeping her there for so long.

"No," repeated the resident, "We want to keep you here for some tests to figure out what caused you to fall."

"I tripped. Now can I go home?"

"What does your car look like?" I piped in uselessly.

My selfish concern being that a mostly blind, 86-year-old, recent stroke patient, looking out of the corner of her right eye, was careening down the same roads where I biked. As if I, of all people, needed any help meeting disaster on wheels.

But before I could ask to check her driver's license, a code was called—fortunately right there in the ER. I ran into the adjacent room while the resident finished with our stroke patient.

In the adjacent trauma room, an elderly man who had just arrived in the ER, lay unconscious on the exam table. We immediately started CPR, but selfishly, despite our resuscitation efforts, he did not get any better.

The patient had been examined at a nearby hospital earlier that same morning for abdominal pain. He had been sent home diagnosed with an upset stomach, which the doctors had told him was "probably not appendicitis."

When the patient turned ghostly white on the ride home from the first hospital and passed out, his son pulled into our ER. We tried everything possible to get his blood pressure and pulse back, but at some point, the doctor in charge made an assessment that nothing was working, and we arrested our efforts.

The decision of when to stop resuscitating a patient is a difficult one and often seemed to depend on the case at hand—at times feeling somewhat subjective. Sometimes it literally depended on whether the family was watching our efforts; in which case we might keep the CPR going a few extra minutes. But this patient hadn't looked well upon arrival, sporting an unhealthy alabaster white pallor and showing no signs of recovering, so we stopped relatively quickly.

It turned out he had a ruptured aortic aneurysm in his abdomen and had lost most of his blood supply to internal bleeding. There was nothing we could have done. The first hospital ER had made an error. They might have saved him with an emergency surgery, but even that was questionable, and he would likely have died there instead.

As we stood debriefing the case and the mistakes made from the other hospital, I learned that another patient had just been incorrectly transferred from the ER and admitted to our hospital floor where he was resisting the administration of IV medicines whilst pleading that he was not really that sick at all.

Not a great start to the hospital day. I could see the headlines, *"Hospital narrowly dodges 'I'm not dead yet' legal battle."*

THE NEXT EVENING ON MOLE DUTY, AS I CRUISED BACK INTO THE labor and delivery area, a very distraught Dr. Tom, the resident covering OB that night, ran up to me requesting my permission to leave the hospital. He asked if I could cover him for a few hours because his son was in the emergency room at the children's hospital with a cold. He assured me that everything was very quiet on the labor and delivery deck, only one woman in labor, and he took off.

I had just sat down in the labor and delivery lounge room to call the ER about admitting a patient, when a nurse ran in asking, "John, can you scrub in to assist on the C-section?"

"C-section?"

Apparently, Dr. Tom failed to include several key facts when he left. Minute details such as the solitary patient happened to be a sick woman being rushed into the operating room. Given that I was supposed to be responsible for all the other residents in the hospital, I decided to call the junior resident and tell her I'd be in the OR if she needed help.

"Oh. Well, I'm here with the dead Greek guy." She responded.

"What dead Greek guy?" I asked.

"I can't pronounce his name properly."

At this point the relevancy of how accurately she could or could not pronounce his name escaped me. I just wanted to know if we were responsible for him no longer being alive. I did find it interesting that mere seconds after being asked to help deliver a baby into the world, I learned of a deceased Greek gentleman— circle of life for you *Lion King* fans.

I did put in a stellar C-section performance and treated myself to the juice and cookies stocked in the OB ward. It was often that simple treat, elementary school juice and cookies, that got you through the late hours, long days and continuous flow of patients. And speaking of continuous flow, the nights of mole duty eventually ceased (I was too sleep deprived to recall or record that moment) and I headed off into the exciting world of urology and incontinence (the patients, not mine).

UROLOGY

VIAGRA & VASECTOMY POETRY JAMS

Every family practice resident in our program was compelled (i.e., forced) to spend an entire month working on a urology team. I can already hear you asking "Urology? Forsooth, what pray tell makes urology important enough to warrant a month-long required elective?"

Incontinence.

That's right, that single word makes urologists very popular.

Nobody wants incontinence.

Or Erectile Dysfunction.

Nobody wants that either. (*At least I didn't.*)

Two more words drawing patients to urologists.

So, the fear and surprise of three words, incontinence and erectile dysfunction, explained why we were required to spend time on a urology rotation.

And *prostates*! Four—four words—for all you Monty Python Spanish Inquisition fans, highlighting why we needed to be well versed in urology: *Incontinence, erectile dysfunction,* and *prostates.*

Once again, I found myself fortunate enough to be training with a hard-working, amazingly talented, passionate-about-medicine physician. This urologist represented the polar opposite of where anyone envisioned my medical career heading: he was absolutely dedicated to the practice of medicine. Full stop. Meanwhile, I sent emails to friends questioning if I should leave residency training with only eleven months left because I wanted to make films.

I decided not to reveal my introspective queries to this ex-Marine, very serious, all-star urologist. I also chose not to disclose that I tried, usually unsuccessfully, to work as an actor on the side to help pay the bills. All he wanted to talk about was urology.

Even before this so-called required elective ("elective" because we were allowed to find an outpatient urologist willing to train us rather than working for the hospital urology service), I had phoned this particular doctor asking his urologic advice for some of my clinic patients. He had always been polite enough to not only call me back (something many physicians did not do), but to also talk with me as though I was a colleague and we were spitballing how best to treat our patient's issues. Most doctors I called to consult treated me like an inconvenient plebe.

I realize that all doctors are quite busy, and it takes time to call back a resident to answer consult questions. But the residency training programs are part of teaching hospitals and so it was the doctor's jobs to teach the medical students and residents. They were paid to do so.

This urologist however, working in his own private clinic, was outside our hospital system, so technically it wasn't even his job to talk to me; he was just polite enough to take time to call me back and share his urologic advice and wisdom. So, I was grateful that he was willing to accept me into his practice to increase my urology knowledge over the course of the month.

Besides common etiquette, I learned a few things during our time together that stuck with me: First, how to properly perform rectal exams to evaluate prostate issues. Second, handing out Viagra samples made patients very happy. Third, one of his seventy-five-year-old female patients with incontinence turned to me and said, "The golden years? They ain't so golden."

Given the huge volume of people we saw with incontinence, I had to agree. Wetting my pants on a regular basis was not something I looked forward to revisiting firsthand. I was mildly consoled knowing that women were forced to confront incontinence far more often than men, and usually at an earlier age.

Male readers don't breathe too deep a sigh of relief, nor stand and cheer just yet.

In exchange for that small gender-based advantage in the piss-your-pants category, men were given a prostate. Prostates do nothing but cause problems. If you're a guy and you live long enough, you're going to have prostate problems. Live even longer and there's a good chance you'll end up with prostate cancer.

The prostate is bad for multiple reasons: First, annual prostate exams. Enough said, there are better things to be doing with your time. Second, not being able to urinate when the prostate enlarges —which it will. Third, having to get up multiple times every night to go to the bathroom for the same reason. Fourth, you may one day need to have your prostate roto-rootered via the urethra. This prospect, alone, started causing me insomnia.

And the next time you're bent over in the doctor's office with his or her gloved finger palpating your prostrate to evaluate it for cancerous nodules, one question you might toss out should conversation wane, "If you can only feel twenty-five percent of the surface area of my prostrate, what's the point of this exam if there could be a cancerous nodule on the other seventy-five percent?"

So, you see ladies, maybe incontinence ain't so bad after all.

Urology was another medical arena where ignorance might have been blissful. Watching prostate surgeries was brutal. Learning about urethral strictures, little areas where the urethra had some damage and had developed scar tissue, which lead to the dreaded roto-rooter, followed by peeing blood for a month, was just awful material for nightmares.

But we men want our plumbing to work and to work well. Which is why everyone applauded, very loudly, the arrival of Viagra and all the other similar drugs to treat erectile dysfunction. My friends in urology residencies, self-proclaimed "Dick Doctors," loved their lives, knowing full well that they would have a long line of patients waiting on their doorsteps as we men aged and needed help urinating and attaining healthy erections.

So yes, my time in urology was mostly spent handing out Viagra samples and performing rectal exams. However, I did learn a few other pearls of wisdom: first, guys should have two orgasms a week in order to prevent the prostate from getting overfilled, topped out, swollen and more enlarged than we want—which could increase the previously mentioned prostate problems.

Secondly, you can fracture your penis. Yes. This was shocking news. It occurred during intercourse and was apparently quite painful, usually requiring abstinence for several months—which made complying with the first pearl of wisdom more difficult. There were definite problems with being aware of these harrowing medical possibilities.

Which, changing topics quickly, reminded me of a patient in my clinic who came in for a back strain months later. The truth finally came out that her back injury had occurred while making love with her husband the night before.

"I'm never trying that position again," she chuckled, "and I'm not telling you what it was, either." Which only piqued my interest further. So, if you, patient with the sexually strained back, are reading this book, perchance, and want to send an anonymous email, my inquiring mind still wants to know what in the world you were doing.

I OPENED THE CHAPTER BY MENTIONING INCONTINENCE AS THE reason many female patients phoned a urologist. But the doctor I worked with did not specialize in treating incontinence, so we didn't see many patients in that category. Instead, let's jump to the second reason I mentioned for needing urology training, Erectile Dysfunction.

Erectile dysfunction (ED) deserves its own book, being a subject close to our hearts and groins and increasing in notoriety with celebrities supporting Viagra and other ED drugs . Magazines and television commercials trumpeted the message that erectile dysfunction is common to almost everybody who camps, plays football, races cars, or gets married—and if you treat ED with that little blue pill, then you can strut through your workplace with a smile and swagger that fellow office people will undoubtedly notice.

The advertisements most certainly wanted to make it look easy for a patient to walk into their doctor's office, discuss the uncooperative subject, and walk out smiling, with nights of passionate bliss dancing in their heads. As a physician I only *wished* patients would walk in and tell me why they were actually in the office. I would have given out free samples of any drug of choice for such a straightforward office visit. In general, it seemed that most men did not like going to the doctor's office for any reason whatsoever, and when they were there, they didn't like to admit why they had come in, especially if it was to put on record that they were not quite the man they thought they used to be.

When I asked male patients what they were in the clinic to discuss, I swear half of them replied, "My wife made me come." An answer that, sexual innuendos aside, did nothing to answer my question.

More often than not there was a good reason that a patient's partner had sent them to the doctor. Perhaps they were sick with pneumonia, had lopped off their finger, or were having symptoms of heart failure. But erectile dysfunction, being a somewhat embarrassing problem to many men, was more difficult for patients to bring up than a sore throat, although perhaps easier to ask about than anal warts.

I should mention that a small number of patients also chose to overcompensate for their erectile chagrin by walking into the office and announcing outright to everyone in the clinic, including the receptionist, other patients, and goldfish in the waiting room aquarium, "I'm here for that little blue pill. I sure hope the doc has samples of that blue pill!"

People really liked the blue pill. Say "the blue pill" and people know exactly what you're talking about by color reference alone. I expect to one day open a box of crayons with my kids and discover that Crayola makes a "Viagra blue" crayon.

When Viagra arrived, it was *the* hot commodity. Friends asked if I could get them samples and residents wrestled over the drug rep's free ties and pens emblazoned with the *Viagra* logo—apparently the pens were a super popular item on eBay, selling for big money. It was a fun pill to prescribe, and you had to be careful with how quickly the samples ran out. I made sure to always save a box for one of my regular patients, an elderly gentleman named Donald (who you will hear more about in later chapters) who was refreshingly upfront in his requests: "Hey Doc, I'm thinking of visiting my lady friend, *you know*, the judge, next week. Could I get some of those blue pills?"

I didn't know the judge, but usually found Donald's stories entertaining and in no way wanted to hinder him bringing me amusing tales of his exploits with the magistrate.

Which brings me to … a certain conversation. At some point during an annual checkup we were taught that doctors should ask every male patient if they were having problems in their sex life. Such problems could be a sign of depression or perhaps a physical health problem, like diabetes. The majority of men under the age of sixty-five usually replied that everything was fine, regardless of whether things were working as well as flaccid Jell-o or even if that had been the actual reason that they had scheduled an annual exam in the first place. Older men might chuckle "Well, things don't work quite the same as they used to."

So, quite frequently, consistent with the usual patient game of, "Guess why I'm really here," the actual reason for the visit was revealed via the "door handle" technique. A wily physician would end the visit, place his or her hand on the room's door handle, then glance back at the patient one last time.

At this critical junction the patient had a moment to decide if they would let the visit end, or quickly blurt out the real reason why they were there to avoid having to make another appointment. "Excuse me, I had one more question..."

Of course you did.

And then you knew that they were finally going to discuss the real reason for the visit besides the curveball concerns with a blister, not sleeping well, a sore elbow, or a mild cough that had resolved itself seven weeks ago. The "door handle" technique was the model of inefficiency, as you now had to conduct a second visit that was often longer than the initial one. Yes, the door handle technique gobbled up precious time, but it was a remarkably effective strategy that we were instructed to use.

During my intern year in clinic, I had met Francis, a patient sent in by his wife for a routine physical exam—despite his being thirty-two years old and quite healthy. His exam was normal, and we ended by discussing some basic health issues.

Then I put my hand on the door and heard, "Excuse me, one more thing…"

The first forty minutes together had been wasted fluff leading up to this real concern: he could not attain an erection with his wife. I was a relatively new resident on the lookout for any elusive and dangerous ailments and I quickly recognized that while his impotence was quite concerning to his social life, I needed to question him to see if there might be other signs or symptoms heralding some terrible disease, like a nervous system problem due to a huge tumor developing on his spine.

I left to discuss his case with an attending physician, which all first-year residents were required to do with their patients. Then I returned to Francis armed with all the questions I'd forgotten to ask, all pertaining to his sex life.

Eventually, after hearing more about his sexual history than I ever wanted, I discovered several interesting and salient points. Importantly for Francis, he was able to attain an erection. In fact, he looked at me like I was the world's biggest idiot for even asking, replying: *"Of course I can get a hard-on!"*

Well, that penile tidbit alleviated my concern for the growing spine tumor. Furthermore, not only was he capable of achieving an erection by himself, but he was *also* very capable of attaining and using a healthy erection with the woman with whom he was having an affair. Just no erections showing up for use with his wife.

He opted to try some little blue Viagra pills for intercourse with his spouse—and much to her supposed satisfaction, everything worked fine.

It took several more meetings to finally convince Francis that maybe, just maybe, the erectile dysfunction issue had something to do with guilt and anxiety about having an affair—regardless of which, he was happy to just keep popping the blue pills to keep his wife happy when necessary.

See, medicine often involves minor detective work.

Another ED patient, a giant Tongan fellow I examined, was in the clinic for a wide host of problems which all led up to me turning the door handle and hearing, "Hey Doc, I can't get my stick up."

He had been a professional boxing trainer and had taken quite a few hits to the head and body. He was also quite obese, which made me concerned that he might have undiagnosed diabetes; a disease that could cause nerve issues and lead to erection problems.

He assured me, however, that the reason he couldn't attain an erection was that his cell phone had been in his front pants' pocket when it rang one day. The phone's vibration, *not* diabetes, was the source of his inability to get his stick up.

He'd started wearing the phone on his chest pocket instead of in his pants and everything was improving—but he thought he could be better in bed with some of those blue pills.

Despite his expert medical assurances that he did not have diabetes, I decided to cover my ass by ordering some blood tests to check. He politely declined, promising me that the phone was responsible for his issues.

If I missed a diagnosis of diabetes, my attending physician would not be impressed. Furthermore, if that error led to a lawsuit and my medical defense was that the patient had vowed that his erectile dysfunction was due to his phone ringing and not diabetes, then I would be medically mocked and have my license revoked.

Hmmm.

In exchange for the magic blue pills, I insisted he agree to the blood tests.

He sullenly agreed—but eventually went home smiling with Viagra samples.

I will admit, every patient walking out of the clinic clutching a packet of Viagra samples in their hand did so with a giant goofy grin.

When my Tongan boxer returned a week later, I informed him that his tests had all been normal.

He shook his head and laughed at me: "I told you so, it was just my phone." I smiled back and shrugged, knowing I had done the right thing, that a semi-punch drunk, elementary-school-educated guy's theory that his phone caused ED was ludicrous. I handed him a full prescription for Viagra and made a mental note not to keep my cell phone in my pants pocket.

FOR THOSE OF YOU WHO READ *PLAYING DOCTOR PART ONE*, YOU might recall that I had my own urological story, when I freaked out about a spider bite on my penis—and you might be wondering if there's anything else I'd like to over-share with you? I do! And this time it's from a group of my friends who used the opportunity of my vasectomy (many years down the road) to compose poetry in honor of the procedure.

I should add that when I went for the required initial evaluation, I walked into the very nice and modern Urology clinic where a cute and friendly female receptionist smiled at me and handed me some paperwork to fill out.

I sat down and started filling out the usual: *name, address, insurance, etc.* Then I got to the important question, *Reason for today's visit: _____.*

And I, a doctor of 15 years at that point, could not, for the life of me, recall what the procedure was called. I looked around; I tried clearing my brain. Nothing. Nada. The word "vasectomy" had completely vanished from my brain. I sat, unwilling to go ask the receptionist the name of the procedure for at least ten minutes. I finally wrote down: *"I'm here for the surgery where you prevent me from having more kids."*

Well done, Dr. John, your time on urology was well spent. Tell me there's not some powerful Freudian shit our brains are capable of pulling off.

So here is the email poetry jam that awaited me fresh from being neutered:

SUBJECT: RE: AN ODE TO JUANDO'S UNDERCARRIAGE
(NOTE: "Juando" is my nickname out here)

AND MORE BABIES WE KNOW THEY NO FURTHER WANTS,
   All the more reason to snip that poor shvantz.

So from the rafters Juando's speedos now hang,
Virility past tense with that neutered wang!
(Scott, esq. of the lung collapsing and multiple arrests fame)

SUBJECT: RE: AN ODE TO JUANDO'S UNDERCARRIAGE

Don't forget to clean said pipes afterwards.
Or ye might have more visit to the maternity wards.
Here's to Juando's ol' severed member
And the day he'd rather not remember.
(Rachel, Scott's wife, who had been a better clinician than me
during the collapsed lung incident)

THIS TALK ABOUT VAS IS PLAIN CRASS.
    It's sarcasm, teasing and sass!
    While poor John can just sit, (fearing a shit),
    You people just laugh and harass.
    (Katherine F. (neighbor))

REMEMBER THAT CONFERENCE IS NEAR.
    (Tuck your garments into your brassiere)
    Joseph Smith would be sad for the vas that he had
    Procreation is why we're all here!
    (Hugh, Katherine's husband)

WITH FRIENDS LIKE YOU, WHO NEEDS A VAS,
    John's procreating days have now come to pass,
    "Neutered," says he; "Free," says we,
    now we toast to his testes with a glass!
    (My wife)

36

. . .

A LIMERICK

A decision was made "no more kids for thee"
The last thing you need is more progeny
The vas deferens you must ligate
Then you can feel free to copulate
But today sit on a bag of frozen pea
(Thomas, Irish Orthopedic surgeon friend)

A HAIKU FOR JUANDO

So long to the Vas
Now like aging yellow lab
Fuck with abandon!
(Otto, university friend)

I HAVE GREAT FRIENDS.

MY EVENTUAL REPLY:

I SEE THE EMAIL LIST HAST GREW,

something my penis for days will not do,
being neutered was the day's fate, now beers and movies do
await;
The World's End is first film to load;
its title seems most apropos.
Xoxo (sterilely) Wando

Outside the world of impotence and incontinence, I still had patients to see in my clinic. That month the one person I remembered well was a sweet eighty-two-year-old woman named Ruth.

I'd first met Ruth several months ago. She'd come into the clinic for a follow-up visit after being treated in the hospital for pneumonia. During her time in the hospital, a CT-scan had revealed a mass in her chest, and it was recommended that she see a pulmonologist to discuss treatments for what was almost certainly lung cancer.

I merely needed to check that she was still alive (which I quickly ascertained from her ability to walk into the clinic), and then refer her to a pulmonologist who would look into her lungs, literally. I made it very clear to Ruth and her daughters that she absolutely must follow up with the lung specialist.

Ruth did not appear to be the brightest ray of sunshine, as she was not even the tiniest bit perturbed by what I was telling her. In fact, I was the only person in the clinic room that seemed the remotest bit concerned about this likely diagnosis of lung cancer.

I forgave Ruth for being flighty; she was, after all, eighty-two years old and recently released from the hospital, where pneumonia had reduced the normal level of oxygen flowing to her brain. I could find no similar excuses for the blank stares reflected in her daughters' eyes.

I repeated that it was very, *very* important that they make an appointment with the lung doctor, whose name and number I handed to them on a piece of paper. I explained again that their mother likely had a tumor in her lung and that the pulmonary doctor needed to establish what type of tumor it was so he could treat her properly. They continued to stare at me blankly, more blankly than the word could ever imply.

"So… does she still have *ammonia*?" one daughter finally asked. (Many patients, for reasons I can't discover, have a fetish for calling pneumonia, *ammonia*)

Much as I wanted to start playing Henry Higgins, I did not believe this to be the time to correct lazy tongues or brains. Instead, I went through the whole problem, one more time, about the likelihood of their mother dying from cancer if they did not get her to the appropriate doctor for evaluation and treatment. After I received one more set of numbed stares, I grabbed back my paper, phoned the pulmonary physician's office and made the appointment for her myself. I then told Ruth and her daughters exactly where to go and on what date, handing the typed information to them on a piece of paper. I even made them read it back to me to make sure they could read and understand it.

Whew.

One month later, Ruth, done up very nicely in a blazer and hat that looked like she was headed to the Kentucky Derby, came to see me for a minor cold. She told me she had a slight cough but assured me that it was just a cold. Her neighbors, however, had insisted that she come see me because she was coughing up blood.

I asked about her visit to the pulmonologist.

"Oh, I didn't need that," she replied.

"Yes. Yes, you did," I told her. "Remember I told you how important that was?" She smiled sweetly as I rampaged on, "Ruth, I am worried that this little cold you have, where you cough up blood and feel short of breath, well, that could be the cancer. This is important, Ruth. Ruth? Do you understand?"

But she just sat smiling at me the whole time, as though we were enjoying a pleasant conversation about the weather. She assured me all over again that it was just a cold, that it was silly of her to come in and waste my time, and that maybe she could just use some cough medicine. I don't even think she was in denial; she was so genuine and sweet.

I decided I better have my attending come in and talk with Ruth, as I was sure to derive yet another reprimand if the staff saw that a patient had died from lung cancer and that the physician

39

somewhat responsible for her health care (that's me) had written off the lung mass and coughing up blood as a "little cold."

I could already hear their critique of my patient care: "So, you treated lung cancer with cough syrup?"

"Yes, but the patient promised me it was just a cold."

"Did you see the CT that said she had a mass in her lungs?"

"Yes. But you're not listening, she told me it was a cold."

My attending that day entered the room and repeated my same blunt warnings to Ruth. Ruth continued smiling and finally agreed she would at least go see the lung doctors to hear what they had to say.

And that was that.

I never heard back from Ruth and assumed the pulmonary team had taken over her care.

Until one day my pager buzzed. I received a call from another attending at the hospital telling me, "Ruth was admitted here last night with pneumonia and since your name was on her chart, I thought you should come in and see her."

I was on a relaxing rotation at the time, a rotation that allowed me several weeks away from the hospital and its smell, but fine, I reluctantly agreed to go see her, the patient I had seen only twice before, and who ignored my advice anyway.

I walked up the well-known stairs to the fourth floor of the hospital that I had spent more time inside than I cared to remember and went into Ruth's room.

There she was, lying in bed, happy to see me. She immediately started apologizing, "I didn't want you to see me like this! I haven't had time to do my hair. But it's sweet of you to be here. I told everyone here I have the best doctor in the whole world. And that's you. Dr. Lawrence."

On and on she continued with the compliments, and I could only think, *Best doctor? Shit, I've let her sit home with lung cancer.*

She admitted she never went to see the lung specialist.

I told her she looked great and that I would see her later that week in the clinic; I thought about what little I had done. She was discharged home the next day.

Now, several months later, during my urology elective, I sat in clinic talking with the same attending that had called to tell me that Ruth was in the hospital. He asked if she'd been back to see me since being discharged. I hadn't heard from her and decided to have her chart brought in to see if anybody else had examined her.

Twenty minutes later I returned from seeing a patient. Ruth's chart lay on my desk, waiting for me.

A yellow post-it label was stuck on the front of her red chart with the words, *"Deceased 07/02/01."*

Time and my heart stopped.

Maybe it was the cold and objective simplicity of that note, the finality.

I'd eventually recognized that Ruth had never wanted any big invasive medical treatments—whether because she was scared, or just did not want it at her age. I had felt really frustrated with her for not doing what I wanted, for not following my sage advice. And she died anyway.

And I recalled the last time I saw her, jokingly complaining that her hair looked terrible in the hospital. I thought she had a lot of dignity to carry herself that way all the time. She had the dignity to live and finally die the way she wanted, without unwanted tubes in her lungs, or nauseating medical treatments.

And then time started again, and life went on because I was forty minutes behind on my clinic schedule.

PRACTICE MANAGEMENT AND NEUROLOGY

THE WORLD CHANGES AND I STILL CAN'T PEE OFF MY BIKE

September was going to be a great month. I planned to attend the Telluride Film Festival over the Labor Day weekend. I'd then return for several weeks of a required "Practice Management" course. This class was designed to prepare us for leaving our rosy, albeit thorny, existence in residency, and entering the real world with its business concerns and expectations. I was then scheduled to spend several weeks on a neurology rotation.

But it was September 2001, and nobody's lives went quite as expected.

I returned from the film festival determined to one day premiere a movie I had written at Telluride. I already had a history of enjoying time in that town with friends, working at the medical clinic and volunteering at festivals. And the film festival, an amazing event headlining great films and filmmakers without the pretension of other grand festivals, matched my dream of film-making and storytelling with the town I loved. The dream persists —and I always remember this quotation passed to us by my university graduation speaker, playwright John Guare: "In dreams begin responsibility."

Then I returned for the practice management course and my desire to leave medicine and enter the world of film was bolstered by days of listening to lectures on the business and legal headaches of a career in medicine.

The basic message of the course? You will never earn enough money to survive as a doctor. You will wrangle lawsuits most of your life. You will be forever mired in administrative work instead of actually practicing medicine. You will need to find alternative business opportunities to create enough cash flow to pay off your school debts.

What's not to love?

Several days into this gripping lecture series, whose ill-timed goal seemed to be driving us away from our chosen career path, I received a message to turn on the TV. So I did.

An immediately identifiable building I recognized all too well was burning. I had worked in a law firm directly across the street from that building and its twin for six months, meeting with clients in the now fiery tower.

Then the second plane hit, and I fell to my knees. I was born in New York, and after some early years in England, grew up in New York. And New York was under attack. The country was under attack. It felt as though the world was under attack. And in those first hours and days the uncertain level of destruction and loss of life burned into our hearts and minds.

In those early moments, nobody knew where the flights had originated, only that they were American Airlines' planes. My mother had flown out of a New York airport at 8 a.m. that same morning on an American Airlines flight, not too long before the first plane hit.

Eventually we learned that the flights involved that day had not originated in New York. My mother's plane had been diverted. Of course I felt overwhelming relief that my mother was alive, but it was a muddled emotion. How could anyone feel anything remotely positive knowing the loss of life, of friends in those buildings, of their loved ones, of victims on the planes, and the courage of the people helping each other out of danger, of storming an airplane's cabin to prevent a larger attack. Grief. Dismay. Anger. Frustration. And an inability to do much to help. The nation seemed struck by a wave of depression and every emotion that accompanies it.

Later that week, a large group of friends and myself were headed to the longest one-day bike race in North America, LOTOJA--a ride from Logan, Utah to Jackson Hole, Wyoming, a little over 200 miles. I was not really bicycling too much anymore but didn't want to miss the ride and had started training ten days beforehand.

Before driving to the race, our group shared the moment of silence with the rest of the country to honor the victims of 9/11.

Most of the riders were quite serious about the race and had their partners to support them along the course, handing out food bags and water bottles. I hadn't really dealt with the logistical part of riding 200 miles just yet. At 10 p.m. I called the motel room of one friend who was riding in my same race category, hoping his wife could maybe help out and support me as well by handing out extra food and water on the route.

Now, you must remember that this was pre-smart phone era, so texting, while far more civilized, was not in use. So, my only option besides knocking on their door, was to ring their motel room phone. Apparently, the blaring phone woke not only my friend, but also their newborn, Sam, who had finally fallen asleep. My friends and Sam were rightfully quite annoyed with my calling (Even I'm annoyed with myself as I write these pages, having now experienced the shock and horror of anyone waking your newborn). Fortunately, his wife agreed to help support me.

The ride started with another moment of silence and then we rode into the dark and cold, heading north in the wee hours of the morning. Along the way people stood cheering, waving US flags. What does this have to do with medicine, you ask? On a 200-mile bike ride you need to eat and drink a lot. All that drinking leads to a need for peeing off the bike.

I discovered a personal weakness: I absolutely could not urinate off a moving bicycle. I just could not relax. I jealously observed other riders coasting down hills, their spandex bike shorts pulled over the front of their bike seats, arcing enviable streams of pee into the air with ease and poise. They were obviously keeping their prostate healthy with the mandatory two orgasms a week.

I tried the short over the seat trick—it resulted in a dribble into my shorts followed by the shorts snapping back on me.

I tried coasting and peeing while thinking of moving water, deep breaths.

Finally, overwhelmed by discomfort, when I could barely breathe and absolutely needed to relieve myself, I got off the bike and went to the bathroom on the side of the road for what felt like ten minutes. By the time this blissful bladder purging finished, the bike peloton was a quarter mile ahead of me and I had to sprint furiously, burning all my reserve energy and leg strength to catch them. At which point there was a general consensus to pull over and take a group bathroom break. That was how I spent much of the ride: stopping to pee, then sprinting to catch the group. A demonstration of cycling inefficiency.

At one point however, I decided to sprint ahead of the main group in order to anticipate my need to urinate off the bike. This logistical calculation had one unforeseen outcome. The generous mother of Sam the newborn that I had woken to ask to support me, did not know I had cycled ahead of the main pack. She waited for her husband in the main group of riders. I therefore never picked up my extra water or food—or very possibly that was her subtle revenge for waking Sam the night before?

For no discernible reason, my small break-away group of four riders let me lead continuously while they rode behind in my draft. Eventually, feeling light-headed and with a mouth so dry it felt like I had been gnawing on chalk, I embarrassingly had to ask the three other riders if they had any water to spare. The good side of not having any water was that I did not have to pee at all for the remainder of the ride.

Now, I suppose this peek-behind-the-spandex of my urologic foibles was suited for the previous urology chapter, except there was NO WAY I was ever considering having a drill inserted through my penis so I could pee off a bike. Ok, never say never. Possibly, had I been on my way to becoming a world class cyclist, and if the only thing holding me back from winning the yellow jersey at the Tour de France was my prostate hindering my ability to urinate off a moving bicycle surrounded by spandex clad men flying by at high speed, then just maybe I would have considered such a procedure. But otherwise, there was *no* way I was ever letting that roto-rooter near my urethra, and certainly not enduring such discomfort for the sake of my poor showings at amateur bike races. Not to mention, as you've already surmised from the last two books, my specialty was falling off a bike, not winning races—or apparently peeing from moving objects.

Urologic issues aside, we rode 209 miles, arrived in Jackson Hole, Wyoming for a small feast and I then promptly passed out exhausted. And for those of you wondering how Scott of the collapsing lungs and golden gate bridge bungee-jump arrest was doing in the premiere race group (CAT 1 riders), he placed in the top three of the race, just like he did every year, with or without functioning lungs.

After the race, I returned to work on the neurology service. No call, no weekends, just testing patient's nerves and reflexes, injecting medicine into tight muscles and prescribing pain medicine for headaches. I am sure there was more, but that's what I learned.

The rest of the month was dominated by some relationship

details that I did not find too entertaining—although my friends certainly did as it added fodder to my reputation for being unable to maintain a happy relationship. Recall that I mentioned meeting a lovely woman a few months back? She was also very intelligent and was headed off to start business school. Well, I was somewhat traumatized by long distance relationships after trying to make one work with my high school sweetheart when I went to college. So the moment this woman flew away, something in my primordial lizard brain entered fight or flight mode.

The weirdest thing was that it was probably the healthiest romantic relationship I had ever been involved in—granted, it was only for a few months—but I managed to screw this one up in short time. So perhaps I could be applauded for becoming more efficient? For once I made a clean break, telling her some lame excuses for why I wanted to end things. She listened, told me good-bye and walked away into the airport. I loved her all the more in that moment.

Relationship woes are nothing but depressing to those involved, and mildly diverting (or exhausting) to those on the fringe—so given it was September 2001, let's take some time to talk about treating depression as a primary care doctor.

DEPRESSION IS A TOPIC THAT REQUIRES DISCUSSION AND understanding; it appears in every field of medicine. It was common to treat a lot of depressed people in clinic and September 11th brought aspects of depression into many lives. And now, the Covid pandemic has increased the prevalence of mental health disorders—specifically, anxiety and depression—and as a result, an increase in the rate of suicide. Fortunately, awareness of mental health disorders has increased as well. People seem more likely to seek treatment, and there are now fewer negative connotations historically associated with mental health issues. But depression and anxiety continue to affect a massive number of people in the world, and we need to find better ways to help.

Over the years in practice, I've lost track of the number of people who confessed to me that they had placed a gun to their head (not figuratively), and then heard their kid calling and put it back down. How do people deal with that life? Sometimes they see their doctor.

We all deal with loss and grief during our lifetime, and we all have injuries of one kind or another. Some deal with chronic illnesses, all of which can lead to depression. Some people are depressed, whether from genetics, hormones, disposition, life events, or just being human. It's out there, a very prevalent, prickly and tough problem for people, their loved ones, and often their doctors.

My parents divorced when I was young. My grades plummeted, I felt isolated, without friends, and asked to leave school for stomachaches almost every week. Nobody ever diagnosed me as depressed. I thought about hurting myself, not because I was sad, but to show my parents the pain they were causing. Fortunately, I never acted on those impulses. But at the time I refused therapy, scoffed at family counseling (I was twelve years old and therefore knew everything), was never offered medicine (would not have taken it) and would've mocked the term "depression." But was there any doubt of the diagnosis? You just dealt with it. Carry on.

Except you had only to look at my flailing relationships over the following decades to assess how well I handled that recovery. I learned to wall up emotions and focus on projects outside personal wellbeing—healthy sublimation has its place. Years later and with the help of therapists, my own relationships became healthier as I accepted a modicum of self-worth. But that was because I finally wanted to face my own internal strife and mental well-being in the face of repetitively unhealthy relationships that floundered due to my own lack of healthy skill sets.

At the same time, I had dated wonderful, creative, intelligent, athletic, successful women with everything in the world going for them, who also struggled with depression. And it drove me crazy. I was dealing with my own insecurities and issues and was frustrated at being ill-equipped to help them properly. I wanted to support them, but nobody can "cure" a depressed person, nobody can make another person become happy when they are dealing with true depression.

Nick Hornby wrote the book, *ABOUT A BOY*, and in the film version, Hugh Grant's self-indulgent character perfectly delivers a wonderful line, telling Toni Collette's chronically depressed character, "And that crying thing, let's get that fixed." Anybody who has dealt with depression or somebody with depression, only wishes it could work that way.

We have all experienced depression. Well, if you have lived consciously, you've had moments of depression: maybe it was the breakup with a person you really loved or perhaps it was the death of a loved one. All of life's great stressors can trigger depression: jobs, relationships, moving, life, death, paying the bills, wondering what you've done with your life, the old adage that "Shit happens." And sometimes there isn't a trigger at all; someone is just depressed.

When people feel depressed, they may show up at the doctor's office wondering what to do. Either way, we're fortunately entering a time when more people are supportive and aware that help is available.

I will admit, early on, it was tough for me to face patients with depression because, as I said, I couldn't handle it too well in my own life. I wanted so badly to help patients, because my role, I thought, was to fix or heal people. Depression is, however, a complex issue to properly handle over time; there's no way it can be adequately addressed during a fifteen-minute clinic visit. It was impossible for someone like myself, who, flippant though I might sound in these pages, felt a connection to most patients I encountered—whether emotionally empathetic, or just wanting to help them due to their seeking my help as a patient.

While certainly not the brightest crayon in the box, I could listen well and emotionally interpret what patients were going through, and perhaps what they needed. And you had to allow enough of a connection to develop trust.

But you also had to be careful. Many times, in listening to the story of a depressed patient, empathy for their hurt drew you into their world, their pain. Exhaustion, or tears, or sympathetic fatigue might creep in and prevent you from doing your job well. As a caretaker you almost had to put up an emotional wall to avoid getting too close; you needed to maintain a boundary.

It was a bit of a paradox: part of the job was getting close, almost intimate, with every patient who wanted to connect—whether with laughter, or knowing you were listening—while retaining professional distance. We needed to reach a balance between being too close—which came with a host of issues, like visits extending too long—and being too abrupt, which was some-times needed after taking too long with a previous patient.

It was easy to say, "Here are some anti-depressant medications and here, some pills to help you sleep. Go see a therapist and see me in a month after the anti-depressants kick in." But that person had to return to their life and still face their misery or sadness.

And when people are depressed, they are not very open to hearing questions about foods they are eating, or recommenda-tions to exercise—key elements that can affect a person's mood. Typically, in our traditional medical clinics, if patients come to see a doctor, they want, and often need, some sort of medical treat-ment, beyond suggestions for lifestyle change. You've perhaps noted that I mention my own interest in biking (despite the acci-dents) and running—while I enjoy being active, I also know exer-cise has served me well as a healthy way to diffuse angst, stress and to ward off spiraling into depression when things get tough. Everyone has their own way of handling rocky emotions and it's so hard to know why one person is more traumatized or why one event is more painful than another.

ONE DEPRESSED PATIENT I TREATED IN CLINIC WAS A VERY successful and handsome thirty-something guy who had just been dumped by his girlfriend. This patient, with everything in the world going for him apart from this recent breakup, was unable to eat, sleep, or get through the day. Relationships end every day, but he was an absolute wreck. I've been there too—but I'll save that story for another chapter.

Another patient, Doug, came to see me after a series of life stressors got him down; he had lost his job, lost his relationship, and moved back home with his parents.

We were trained to ask certain questions of depressed people:

Have you thought about hurting yourself?

Have you tried to hurt yourself in the past?

Do you have a plan to hurt yourself?

Depending on patient's answers, we were supposed to take the responsibility of admitting that person, against their will, into a psychiatry unit until they were not dangerous to themselves.

Doug had already made one attempt to commit suicide before visiting me. Since he was crying to me in the exam room, you may correctly assume that his attempt had failed. When a big tough-looking man breaks down in front of you because his wife left him, it's damn hard, as a member of the human race, not to be affected. That's true when most any patient breaks down in front of you. Anyway, Doug had already attempted suicide, and now seemed pretty shaken up by his entire life. But something about the way he presented himself made me think he really wanted to crawl out of the dark place where he now found himself.

I asked Doug to come back to the clinic to see me quite frequently those first weeks and gave him the right to call a resident at night (we had someone on-call to answer such calls and tell people to go to the emergency room) if he needed to. I sat and talked with him about life, books to read, and what he was going through. We were not therapists, and we always recommended that patients follow up with a trained social worker, psychologist, or psychiatrist, but Doug seemed to feel safe talking with me—so I thought it important to maintain that open dialogue.

All the while, each visit with Doug made my patient schedule fall further behind—but I figured maybe I was helping this guy forgo any further suicide attempts. He had days when he thought about trying again, which made me scared thinking he might not show up for a meeting one day because he had gone through with it properly this time. But he started some medication for the depression, and some medicine to help him sleep, and slowly he clawed his way back into life.

A few months later he had been offered a job but needed a signed physician's note stating that he had been prescribed a controlled medication. The problem was that the meds he had taken did not belong to him. He explained that he had taken a few of his mother's pain pills for a sore back he developed after doing yard work at his parent's house. This potential job, a major step in Doug reaffirming purpose in his life, was on the line unless I could write a note that stated I had actually written this narcotic prescription for him.

If I wrote the note, I would be lying about prescribing a controlled substance. There were no office notes to back up this false claim. Writing this note would be illegal, a felony, and if called out, I could face serious ramifications, possibly loss of license and dismissal from my residency program. I considered the circumstances, and the person and faxed a note stating I had prescribed Doug pain pills.

Three months later he still had the job and all things considered, was doing great. He had his down days and came to see me if necessary.

That Christmas I received a card from Doug with a gift certificate to a very nice restaurant. At that time I was seriously questioning my role, if any, in medicine. The residency program's perception of me was variable at best, with a large cabal believing me a poor and uncommitted physician due to my honest quandary of whether or not to even practice medicine. Then I received Doug's card with the words, and this is verbatim as I kept the note:

"Dr. Lawrence, Thank you for going far above the call of duty. I am very happy and I look forward to the future every day. It's a wonderful thought to know Doctors like you are helping people when we need you most. I will be forever grateful to you, for all you have done for me. Thank you, Doug."

I wanted to send a copy to all my critics in the residency program, all those folks who voted to put me on secret executive probation. Far more importantly, at a time when I was questioning even finishing residency, Doug's words reminded me that I was helping people, and those words helped me complete the whole damn thing. Thank you, Doug.

But cases of depression were everywhere, and we did not always have the time necessary, or the skills needed to help.

Lily was a woman that came into my clinic years later to be treated for a strange rash that had developed on her face and hands. It was a nasty infection that required several weeks of antibiotics. She was a very friendly woman and I assumed she had a nice normal life.

A few weeks after that initial visit, she came into the clinic to follow up on the rash, which was healing quite well. She was a little tearful. I didn't know why, so I just waited for her explanation, guessing she might be feeling slightly depressed.

Lily hinted at a rough life and her muddled words slowly changed into sentences such as, "I have nothing to live for." And "My life sucks." My questions of whether or not she was depressed were apparently answered.

Then she told me, "I have come from the depths of hell." *Well that statement caught my attention.* It turned out she was a single mother who had been homeless. She now lived in a shelter and every day was afraid of going back to her homeless existence. Her ex-husband repeatedly told her youngest boy that he planned to cut her throat from ear to ear.

At this point she broke down, but more from what I could see was genuine terror. Then she admitted she had thought about ending the pain and fear, but she had kids. So, she went to work every day, cared for her kids, and functioned really well. Her kids were the motivation to stay alive and work.

I couldn't change Lily's life, and that wasn't my job. But I could start her on some medicines to make it possible to get through the day without as many tears and have her promise to call me or see me if she ever thinks about hurting herself. Life is precious—and here was a person, coming from the *depths of hell*, functioning better than many of the educated people, people with everything good in their life except a recent breakup (i.e. frequently me). But comparisons are complete bunk, no circumstance can be measured in its level of personally devastating quality.

Options exist—please use them:

National Suicide Prevention Hotline: 800-273-8255 (24/7)

Crisis Text Line: Text SUPPORT to 741-741

National Alliance on Mental Illness: 800-950-6264

Sexual Abuse Hotline: 800-656-4673

Veterans Crisis Line 800-273-8255

EMERGENCY ROOM

MENINGITIS, ABSCESSES AND GUNSHOTS, OH MY!

The attending ER physicians had seen me in action over the last years, and were now willing to let me work more independently—which felt great. It was about time for me to start exhibiting that I knew what I was doing. After all, I would be working as a fully trained doctor in the very near future. So, while I was not exactly boasting about my medical skills, I stepped into the offered independence with a splash of confidence —typically a strong barometer reading for an impending fall.

I previously mentioned two big learning curves during a medical resident's education. The first was during the intern year when you were so completely overwhelmed by learning to work as a doctor that you forgot how to tie your own shoes. The volume and barrage of work that first year produced a learning curve, from medical ignorance to a modicum of competency, which was pretty fantastic. Within one year you learned so much, that you felt reasonably competent in your abilities when you became a second-year resident.

The second year would seem like the most likely place for accidents or mistakes to occur, as confidence was heightened, and the learning still not so great—a potentially lethal combination. But you went through the middle year feeling pretty good, while also having a team of residents and doctors watching your backside; then came the third year.

The reality smashed you right in the face that you were going to be taking care of patients by yourself very soon. Consequently, self-assurance was known to dip. You began questioning some of your medical decisions because you were acutely aware of how much information and skill remained to be learned. Then slowly over that last year the second big learning curve kicked in, as you worked to soak up every bit of education possible.

As a senior resident, you were also forced to expand and solidify your skill base by teaching all the resident teams. Recall the medical school adage for learning a new procedure: *See one, do one, teach one.* If you can properly teach a skill, which is what senior residents should be doing for all their junior residents, it's usually a sign you've learned it well.

I hadn't yet been slapped down with the realization of working in the real world because I was still convinced that I was never going to be a real doctor. I was, however, feeling pretty good about my competency in the ER. Treating a sore throat, laceration, or case of back pain—no problem, I could handle them with a smattering of composure—at least compared to my bumbling earlier years in medicine.

Then one fine ER morning, I strolled into a room to evaluate a patient whose chief complaint was fever. She was a middle-aged woman who appeared miserable, exhibiting the shaky, feverish look of a person with influenza.

Her husband explained that they had just been seen at her regular doctor's office earlier that same morning because she had been feeling quite sick at home. Their doctor had ordered some blood tests and sent her home. On the way home however, she developed a headache and started feeling even worse. So they immediately pulled into our ER for help seeing if anything more serious was causing her to feel so miserable.

While we were casually discussing her symptoms, I could not help but notice that she really did look quite ill. I guessed she had early pneumonia, or some comparably severe secondary illness that often accompanies influenza. Then she mentioned that her headache was worsening and that her fingertips and toes hurt.

Huh. Well these new symptoms sound kind of strange.

I asked the nurse to re-check the patient's temperature. When she did, it was close to 104 degrees. A 104-degree fever (40 degrees Celsius) in an adult is an impressive sign that something serious is affecting the body.

As I continued asking questions, the words "fever and headache" started bouncing around inside my cranium. There are a few red flags not to be missed in the ER, and one of them is the combination of fever and headache, the classic sign and symptom of meningitis.

Bacterial meningitis can kill you—kill you quickly. But we rarely saw bacterial meningitis. Patients usually had some form of viral meningitis and we sent them home to get better with Tylenol and fluids.

Despite this woman's ill appearance, and her symptoms sounding like meningitis, I did not want to overreact by doing anything hysterical for a bad cold. At the same time, prancing around in the hinterland called my brain, was a random story about bacteria being able to trigger clotting complexes to form in the blood. Those complexes could obstruct small blood vessels in extremities, which could make toes and fingers hurt due to a lack of blood supply.

My interior monologue started to dominate the conversation I was having with the patient's husband.

While he was talking, more medical lessons echoed deep in my head—somewhere out there was the scary time frame to properly treat patients with meningitis that involved getting a CT scan, starting IV antibiotics, and doing a spinal tap to save their life.

But wait, hold everything:

Was I supposed to get the CT scan first to make sure there was no aneurysm or bleed in the brain that would cause problems with a spinal tap, and then start the antibiotics?

Except I think time was supposed to be really critical, like do it all in under thirty minutes before the patient died on you?

So was it spinal tap, antibiotics, CT? Clock's ticking, shit...Or maybe it was antibiotics, CT, then the tap...Oh fuck, I don't know.

"Excuse me," I said and walked out of the patient's room.

Suddenly it was black Monday, Greek myth day, pride going before the fall, and my competence had plummeted, any modicum of hubris pancaked flat on the ER's tiled-floor. The recently secure decision maker in me was now flailing, and I was unable to think straight or remember any specific order for treating and diagnosing this sickly patient.

I needed to find the attending physician.

When I found the attending-du-jour, she was on a personal call regarding hotel reservations in Antigua. I sat, trying to be patient, tapping my clipboard, looking around, spinning objects on her desk. She finally scheduled her vacation and raised her eyebrows wondering why I needed to see her. I was, after all, a relatively competent third-year resident and should be able to handle most cases without her help.

I casually stated that I was seeing a sickly-appearing woman with a headache and high fever.

She looked at me a little more concerned, asking, "Well, John, doesn't that sound like meningitis?"

"Yes, that's why I was waiting but you were on the phone and—"

"Get a scan, order the antibiotics and tap her as soon as she's back from CT. What are you waiting for?"

"Uh..."

"Go!"

The patient was immediately whisked away to the CT scanner while antibiotics were ordered. She returned minutes later, and I performed a great spinal tap that would've warranted being hoisted onto shoulders and run around the clinic, except the patient was really sick, and if we could judge by appearances, rapidly worsening.

As soon as the antibiotics arrived from the pharmacy, they were immediately infused into the patient through an IV. Then her bloodwork came back with a frightfully high level of white blood cells (WBCs). This high level of WBCs more than suggested she had something serious going on, likely bacterial meningitis—which we had already assumed and were treating.

At this time, as if we needed more evidence to support the *"something serious is going on"* theory, a new complication cropped up—the patient's fingertips and toes started turning black.

Now I was a bit terrified.

The hospital's Infectious Disease (ID) specialist, a brilliant and genial woman, was out of the hospital at that moment. I quickly phoned every nearby hospital to locate an ID specialist to consult, as this case was getting batshit crazy. None of them answered their phones or paging services—a rush on doughnuts presumably had them all simultaneously detained.

When I finally did get through to one ID guy, he turned out to be a total prick. He told me he did not have time to talk with me since he was not getting paid for his services.

Most physicians are very happy to give advice to aid in the treatment of sick patients; it's why they chose to practice medicine, not to mention this was proving to be a very urgent case requiring immediate treatment advice to save a person's life.

This ID doctor told me to call back if I could not get in touch with anybody else in the Western United States. I told everyone within earshot what an ass this doctor was and to never call him again, ever, for anything.

Finally our hospital's ID specialist called back and was, for obvious reasons, quite concerned about my patient. She gave me a laundry list of medications to start running through the IV, told me to page her if anything changed, and promised to be there as soon as possible.

Around the same time the lab called to say that there were definitely bacteria in the patient's spinal fluid, i.e., we were dealing with bacterial meningitis, but no cultures would be ready any time soon that could tell us what exact breed of bacteria, and what antibiotic would work best for treatment.

Finally, with her toes and fingers turning black, the patient was transported up to the ICU.

The meningitis eventually turned out to be caused by a weird strain of Streptococcus Bovis bacteria. While I was not directly involved in her ongoing care, I kept abreast of what was happening. The worst complication at first was the blackening of her fingers and toes spreading. Her hands and feet turned black as her arterioles (medium sized blood vessels) became obstructed by the complexes that formed in her blood, i.e. clots blocking off blood supply to her extremities.

Infectious disease, ICU, and plastic surgery specialists all consulted each other, debating what to do over the next weeks as the patient became septic (multiple organ systems overwhelmed by infection and going into failure), was intubated, and the flesh of her hands and feet started decaying.

It was a startling case to witness, knowing she had been perfectly healthy two days before I met her. Last I knew, the plastic surgery team thought it was best to amputate most of her hands and feet to prevent any further spread of infection from the dead tissue—but the family was resistant to any amputation.

I began feeling guilty about not having initially reacted quickly enough; perhaps the patient would not be needing amputations if I had been rude and interrupted the ER attending's Caribbean vacation planning. I eventually discussed the case with that same doctor, wondering if the patient might be doing better had I ordered her medications five minutes earlier.

She thought we had done everything correctly. Sometimes patient cases just did not go well. I was sure their doctor, the one who sent them home, was not feeling much better than I did.

I previously wrote about a patient who had been sent home from the V.A. hospital's ER with a bellyache. He felt worse and came into our ER, by which time his blood pressure was almost zero. He died from a ruptured aortic aneurysm on our ER exam table. Mistakes happened. Sometimes bad results happened, and nothing would have stopped them.

The ER doctor then told me that one of my fellow residents was thinking of quitting medicine because she felt responsible for a recent bad outcome.

An otherwise healthy diabetic 23-year-old girl had been admitted from the ER with diabetic ketoacidosis (DKA). This serious condition arises when a diabetic patient's blood sugars elevate to really high levels, leaving the patient feeling sick and confused as the ketones in their body also elevate and their blood becomes acidic. DKA was treated quite frequently in the hospitals and was very dangerous.

Fortunately there were very specific treatment protocols that dictated exactly how to care for patients with DKA. A literate preschooler could order and follow the protocol: hydrate the patient with IV fluids, order hourly blood draws to monitor blood chemistry and acid/base levels, and then slowly lower their blood sugar levels with IV insulin.

The patients were straightforward to care for because you just followed those very precise protocols. But, at the same time, their care was quite tedious because your pager rang every hour to call for lab results and then you adjusted treatment according to the scripted protocols. This specific woman was admitted, treated, and everything fell into place nicely. In the ICU her blood sugar levels were falling appropriately.

Then someone dropped the ball.

Because the patient's physical appearance started to look well and her blood lab values were all improving, they stopped following the protocol, stopped ordering the annoying hourly blood tests, and missed the fact that the patient's bicarbonate level was staying low, i.e. her blood gas levels were still acidic.

Despite looking good, the real danger still existed.

She died later that night.

I had questioned my own desire to stay on as a resident multiple times, and bad outcomes with patients provided some of the most provocative internal debates for not wanting to continue. The resident in that case, after wrestling with her own psyche, continued on and is a fantastic physician.

NOT EVERYTHING IN THE ER DEALT WITH EGO-SHATTERING CASES, or, as I have previously written about, drug-seeking patients. The majority of cases were ones we could take care of properly. One enjoyable aspect of working in the ER was the ability to perform small procedures—and one of the most common ones was, brace yourself, draining infected abscesses.

Later that month I walked into a patient's room and met a very polite twenty-year-old woman sitting with her friend, both looking bashful. She told me that she had some irritation. After beating around the bush for some time I finally asked where she was actually having the "irritation"?

To which she replied, "I wore some polyester underwear a week ago."

An answer that did not really answer my question but was

typical of the unhelpful responses I had come to expect in medicine. It was a game patients liked to play to help evoke my Sherlock Holmes principles of deduction to figure out why they had come to see me. Let's put those powers to work with a truly probing question:

"What kind of irritation?"

"A bump."

This was like pulling teeth.

Still unsure if we were discussing a back zit or a diaper rash I asked, "And where, exactly, is the bump?"

She was twenty years old and must have been slightly embarrassed to be discussing the problem, but at her age I suspected she had a decent knowledge of her own anatomy. Finally she replied that the bump was on her vagina and admitted she was worried about this being an STD.

I asked if she was sexually active—she replied she wasn't, which lowered the risk of an STD. I informed her that the only way to get to the bottom of the mystery would be to take a look at the irritating bump, and I left the room while she changed into a gown.

When I returned with a nurse to be present for the exam, the patient was on the exam table under a sheet. I explained in a very professional manner that I would not do anything sudden, and that I just wanted to look and see what could be causing this irritation. I prided myself on always acting with appropriate decorum, no matter what the patient case.

I folded back the sheet and jerked back from shock. I barely suppressed a gasp, before the words, "My God, I thought you said *irritation?*" escaped my lips.

There in front of me was a baseball-sized abscess oozing pus (Okay, that was gross. Sorry).

"Well, I put some Neosporin on it, and it got worse," she replied.

"Yes, fine, very well," I stammered incredulously. "But you said you had some irritation, this...this is... horrible."

So much for professional decorum.

This poor girl obviously had no sense of the English vocabulary because nobody describes red grapefruit-sized globes of pus as "irritation." Not to mention this disgusting purulent volcano was on her thigh and inches away from anything resembling her vagina—not far enough, however.

I prepared to exorcise and drain this alien on her thigh, cleaning her skin with Betadine, and numbing the area using Lidocaine with epinephrine (epi).

You've likely seen some medical television drama and heard doctors calling for, "Epi, stat!" Well, that's for a different type of emergency.

We use Lidocaine mixed with epinephrine, as the latter drug causes blood vessels to constrict, so the numbing effect of Lidocaine sticks around longer, and with blood vessels constricted, the wound bleeds less. But there were a few essential rules to remember when using this anesthetic mixture.

Since medical school this unbreakable rule was drummed into our heads: *Never ever inject epi into a patient's nose, fingertips or genitals, as the blood supply to these important areas could be cut off when the blood vessels constrict.* It was a question that appeared repeatedly on examinations. Few people would think kindly of you if their nose or penis fell off because you had cut off the blood supply—poor form.

I was not too concerned with treating this patient with epinephrine, as the area I was numbing was not directly on her genitalia. So, I injected her skin and decided to be liberal with the Lidocaine (with epi) because she was in pain. Her skin quickly turned white due to the medicine's vaso-constrictive effect, which was normal.

But the whiteness kept spreading—spreading towards her vagina. I continued watching fearfully as the area of vessel constriction grew. I was trying not to sweat, but I was beginning to consider the consequences of cutting off the blood supply to this area.

Could this possible error result in chemical female circumcision? I had no idea what to do. Massaging her thigh to stimulate blood flow would certainly not appear professional.

Fortunately for all involved, the medicine stopped spreading just shy of disaster and I quickly plunged a sterile dagger into the offending beast. It was gross and I'll spare you the details as there are few medical cases that turn my stomach, but draining abscesses is one of them. I packed the wound with gauze (so it would not, like the Terminator, reform and come back), gave her a prescription for antibiotics and sent her home with a brief anatomy lesson.

Well, that was a somewhat uncivilized story, but I still cannot believe she tried to fake me out with the "vaginal irritation" line.

People do get abscesses and for some unfathomable reason, often chose to watch them enlarge at home. Very commonly we treated IV drug users with abscesses on their arms. They entered the ER with blustery swaggers, often with tattoos covering their bodies, and when I told them that draining the infection would hurt, they laughed in my face, telling me to lighten up, that they could handle pain just fine—the tattoo and history of injecting themselves being evidence of their machismo.

But when I started cleaning out their abscesses, they almost universally (and justifiably) started crying before threatening to kick my ass when I was finished (not justified!). Luckily their friends usually restrained them during the procedure.

The beyond expectations vaginal irritation case turned out to be just the start of that day. The usual patients with colds and pain came to visit and then the full moon rose.

One second, I was suturing together a guy's lacerated thigh, the next I was shocked to my feet by the sounds of agonizing wails echoing through the ER. I ran to the waiting area where a young man, maybe twenty-years old, bawled in pain, holding his leg while several of his buddies helped him into a wheelchair. Blood dripped onto the floor from his jeans.

"I'm shot, I'm shot!" He screamed.

His friends shouted at us to hurry up and save his life, imploring us to rush their gunshot victim friend back to the operating room so that they could run out and go after the guy that had shot him. Which did not sound like a well-advised plan to me.

In the ER you did try to maintain a certain state of unflappable calmness, but their ridiculous vigilante attitude aside, I was kind of excited to check out the bullet wound as we didn't see many of these. All you really did with bullet wounds in the arm or leg was find out what happened and order X-rays after checking what nerves or blood vessels might have been damaged before referring them to surgery if needed.

This poor lad had been in a grocery store parking lot when a guy he didn't even know, *"A Black guy,"* he told us, shot him and ran off. His friends had pursued the guy to no avail.

While we were waiting for this patient's X-rays, a young Hispanic woman wandered into the waiting room; then stumbled outside again, only to return to the foyer and collapse on the floor.

As the nurses rushed to pick up the unconscious woman, the police rushed into the waiting room. They were bringing in a hysterical and bloodied young woman whose boyfriend had just put her face through a glass table.

This last patient did not look too good. She would require glass removal, suturing and social counseling. She was actually more distraught about her relationship than anything else—jumping frenetically up and down between fits of crying from pain, declaring that her boyfriend was an asshole who should be in jail, and explaining everything that was wrong with their relationship.

As far as I was concerned, the guy putting her face through a glass table was all I needed to hear to evaluate their relationship. But she kept complaining over and over about their communication problems and his inability to commit. After several minutes of listening to her talk show banter, my empathy waned as I tried to help lift the now semi-comatose Hispanic woman off a gurney and into a bed.

Meanwhile the X-ray came back on the kid that had been shot and showed that the bullet was not lodged anywhere dangerous. At this point the police started questioning the patient about his attacker. Before the police finished their interrogation however, the victim's dad, who appeared to have arrived directly from winning a Willie Nelson lookalike contest, stormed inside demanding to know where he could find and kill the guy who had shot his son.

Then more police arrived (I did not realize there were so many police in the entire city) holding another patient, this time a guy with bleeding wrists. I went to evaluate the severity of his injuries. It turned out that he had stuck his hands through a glass table when he got mad at his girlfriend and put her face through it.

I let him know that his significant other was in the adjacent room and that she had a few words for him.

He actually seemed like the more normal of the two, had no prior history of any violence and was now rightfully freaked out by the night's hostility. He put on a bravado act that consisted of nervously rambling while handcuffed to the table with policemen surrounding him as I examined his bleeding wrists. As if to display that he still had the ability to make his own decisions, however stupid they may be, he refused to get an X-ray, despite the fact that I could not guarantee that I'd removed all the embedded glass. I could see a cut tendon and thought it medically prudent to know if any glass was still inside this deep cut before I sutured the tendon back together and closed the skin. But suddenly he was medically proficient and informed me that the glass was all out.

I decided to take a break from his verbal ramblings and misguided decision making and headed to see his soon-to-be ex-girlfriend (although I'm sadly willing to bet they were back together again the following week).

As I walked around the corner, however, a young Hispanic man, deathly pale, came rushing inside the ER holding an unconscious toddler with an even paler pallor and a large bruise on his forehead.

I was the only semi-Spanish-speaking medical person in the ER and not great at that, as you have surmised in earlier chapters, but figured I better get this case figured out. The mother had apparently thrown a toy car across the room and accidentally struck the child in the head. At this point, with almost twenty policemen in the ER, accidental child trauma did not go over very well. I had the feeling this guy was completely upfront, honest, and caring for his boy and that what he said was true. But I took care of the medical stuff first and had the boy rushed off for an immediate CT scan of his head while the police brusquely questioned his father.

At this point the police were also starting to get gruff with the bullet wound patient and I heard one of them grilling him, "Why don't you tell me what really happened?"

The kid repeated his story about a "Black guy" shooting him in the parking lot and running off. And the police officer was kind of a jerk, telling him to shut up and tell him the truth. Which the kid vehemently insisted he'd been doing.

Finally the officer asked, "Did you shoot yourself?"

I was shocked at this line of questioning, certainly not the type of thing I typically asked in my interviews. Instead of getting more hostile however, the kid stopped arguing, hung his head and nodded affirmatively.

It turned out he had been holding a loaded pistol while driving with his friends. The gun fired while he was playing with it in his lap. A few inches higher and the resulting situation might have been worse for the patient—albeit rather deserved in my mind after his attempts to blame someone else.

At this point the patient's father went ballistic and started raging at his son's stupidity, promising the police officers he would find and kill whoever had sold his son the pistol. I just kept hoping he would break into a Willie Nelson song.

My shift had ended three hours earlier, but there was too much action to be missed, and I stayed on another two hours to help until the majority of patients had been sent home, all doing fine. That's how much fun you can have working in the ER.

HAIL TO THE CHIEF!

WHERE I GOOD-NATUREDLY AIM TO INSPIRE THE INTERNS—AND THEY ALL LEAVE THE PROGRAM

The ER party skidded to an abrupt halt and the next day I was crowned Chief Resident of the Family Practice Service. I had worked towards this position for years: Chief, Lord, and Emperor of the hospital's daily resident circus. It wasn't a lofty position at all, but with residency victories hard to come by, I planned to make the best of the role.

Over the previous years, my required months on this internal medicine rotation had left me somewhat jaded—more accurately, I hated this service and loathed any time spent on it. As interns, we had all been required to spend three months on this rotation. On my third go-around in the spring of that year, I showed up with a worn-down and admittedly piss-poor attitude. We interns were exhausted by then, having endured months of inpatient rotations with busy call nights and weekends in different hospitals. I anticipated more long days and nights inside the hospital's grim walls, pestering patients about their pesky bowel habits, and viewing it as anathema to whatever meager embers of happiness still resided within me.

So, I already disliked the Family Practice Service and its

accompanying obligation, my nemesis: morning rounds. My dislike of morning rounds was likely a defensive response to being repeatedly put on the spot and fearfully waiting for the entire hospital to see through my naked emperor charade, realizing that I did not know anything about being a doctor. But now I was the chief in charge of morning rounds, and if left to my own desires, would simply jettison rounds altogether. *If only life were so simple.*

Residency programs adore morning rounds, so it would be difficult, impossible actually, to justify my eliminating them. I decided to at least gift my students and residents a better experience than the ones I had grumpily survived. I wanted to somehow make it fun, and if not fun, tolerable and educational. I therefore needed to keep the instructive element, but also create a more bearable environment to set a better tone for the rest of the resident's workday.

If the chief resident and attending set a positive tone in those stressful, under-slept weeks, we could all make it through the morning with some learning and get back to the hand-cramp-inducing institution of writing patient notes and admitting patients to the hospital. Ideally, our leaders would inspire camaraderie to help pull each other through the month of hard work and opportunistic learning—and that was my goal as Chief, provide a positive learning environment that nobody despised.

Why call it *opportunistic* learning? Because learning was based upon whatever roll-of-the-illness dice the population tossed on your call night. If your presence during call nights triggered gastrointestinal bleeds in the surrounding townships, then you became quite adept at knowing what to do and what to order for patients showing up with bright red blood flowing from their rectum. That was a true emergency we discussed in previous chapters.

To even the playing field, in case for example you never had the opportunity to admit your own patient vomiting from pancreatitis, we would repeatedly discuss a variety of differing cases during morning rounds, so you could vicariously work through how to diagnose, evaluate, and treat patients with varying ailments. But really, your best learning opportunities arose from caring for your own patients—you did not forget the cases you personally worked on—especially the ones you screwed up.

And as previously described, rounds were the Socratic teaching method from Hades that almost drove me to hemlock. But the hospital was, despite the jading hours of grunt work, an ivory tower for education where Socratic teaching opened and molded the future minds of health care in this country. Never mind that our Ivory tower was, to say the most, on the fourth floor of a fading white building whose paint was peeling.

Let's take a moment and flash back to my whiny, fatigued, emotionally scarring, third-times-not-a-charm, intern year-family practice service rotation.

FLASHBACK INTERN YEAR:

The ivory tower model tumbled down during the spring of my intern year, starting at the top with our chief resident, Hilda (not her real name), a deservedly burned-out-beyond-charred-muffins, third-year resident who apparently thrived on re-watching *An Officer and a Gentleman* over and over. Hilda was intent on demonstrating that she was a militantly strict educator to us, her peon junior residents. Or maybe she was just a bitchy individual made more so by having spent the last years of her life in hospital settings

Do you see what I mean? Suddenly, I'm turning mean and vindictive. I was obviously a bit fried myself.

Besides my soon-to-be arch-nemesis, the chief resident, our team for the month included: Shelby, a super-friendly, second-year resident with a lovely Southern accent; Greg, another second-year resident, who was openly fed-up and cynical about every aspect of medicine (an attitude I'm quite certain he held before starting residency); a swarthy intern wearing a shabby lab coat with ring-around-the-collar (that's me); and lastly, Erica, a ridiculously anal-retentive, second-year resident harboring delusions that she was Surgeon General to the entire World.

Adding to Erica's savory disposition was her nasty habit of perseverating over every, single, bloody (literally), patient detail—droning on and on until most of us were asleep.

In fact, I stopped trying to stay awake in rounds—which you can imagine went over really well with Hilda. Rather than doze off sitting up, I merely put my head down on the desk and went to sleep any time Erica was talking. Reflecting back, she was the single most brilliantly cagey resident I ever encountered—not only was her blatant ass-kissing applauded by our bosses, but her sleep-inducing presentations were spells that made the rest of us look like dozy, disinterested, weak, and lazy Muppets.

In addition to surviving the gripping chore of examining patients, I was also at that time experiencing some of my then girl-friend's busy surgery chief resident schedule. At some point she had single-mindedly agreed that I would share her call schedule—which she took from home. Therefore, on the few nights I was liberated from the hospital, I was able to experience, firsthand, a continual rancor of ringing pagers, heated phone conversations to the hospital, and her frequent excursions to and from the emergency room—complete with case debriefings when she returned.

The end result was that I almost lost more sleep on the nights when I was supposed to be recovering from call nights than on the actual call nights, themselves, and was therefore absolutely exhausted and shattered during that time period.

Her surgery schedule was significantly worse than my family practice schedule on a regular basis, so I would not dare open myself up to ridicule by admitting fatigue. At the same time, I decided there was no point to drinking coffee on the days I worked in the hospital. What fathomable reason was there for me to be either alert or in a good mood while taking care of patients? I think the last statement accurately (and pathetically) sums up my fine attitude and professional mindset during the final months of my intern year.

The combination however, of increasing exhaustion and lack of caffeine, coupled with redundant patient presentations, all dominated by Erica's desire to prove herself empress of medical minutiae, almost terminated my already tenuous existence in residency.

The rounds started and the futile battle to keep my eyelids open began. Whichever resident had been on-call in the hospital the previous night would kick off morning rounds by presenting a patient they had admitted with an "interesting" diagnosis. Interesting was relative when your options usually included a case of chest pain (typically a heart attack, blood clot in lung, or pneumonia), bleeding from the rectum (maybe an ulcer, but need to rule out colon cancer), or a stroke (call the neurology team).

After months of hearing the same cases, we all knew the catchphrases, knew what was relevant to each case, and just wanted to get through the morning rounds. But Erica made it a point to ensure we all knew that she could vocalize such knowledge better than the rest of us.

And after we worked through the new patient presentation, we would all take turns discussing the patients under our own care.

Greg would start his presentation in his typically cynical and monotone voice, "This is an old woman who came in short of breath and is being treated for pneumonia. She had an X-ray this morning. She's doing better. She'll probably go home tomorrow."

That terse presentation pleased neither the attending, nor the chief resident—and certainly not Erica. Erica would smile at the chief, then convey both their disappointment by completing a gloriously smug shake of the head, eye-roll combo, complete with deep sigh, before interrupting, "Greg, did you see the X-ray?"

Greg would turn to Erica incredulously, "What?"

"If there was an X-ray, you should see it."

"No, I didn't see the X-ray. Did you?"

"It's not my patient, Greg."

"It's not my patient Greg," he parroted back.

"Greg, what was that?" the chief resident interjected to stop the impending residents-gone-wild wrestling match.

"I'm trying to give my report. Can I finish my report?"

Everyone would quiet down as Greg looked at his notes to start again.

"Where was I?" he asked.

"You had just decided not to see your patient's X-ray," added Erica.

"Fuck you," Greg exhaled under his breath.

"Greg!" The chief quickly tried exerting control.

"Sorry. I saw the radiology report. The report said improving."

"That's it?" asked Erica.

"That's it. She's going home tomorrow."

I started grimacing as I saw Erica shake her head, smiling at Greg as she asked, "What were her lab results today?"

"Her labs were normal, Ok? On exam everything was normal."

"I'm sorry," Erica interrupted once again in her sing-songy voice, smiling at the chief as she asked, "Did you mention the TSH level?"

"No, I didn't mention the TSH level."

"What was it?"

"I said all her labs were normal."

"Ok. Then what was her TSH?"

"I didn't get a goddamn TSH."

"Why not?"

"What is your problem?"

"I'm just saying a TSH might be relevant. Just in case."

"Just in case what, you'—?"

"Greg!" The attending physician cut off the escalating fun.

We all knew that you could justify checking a thyroid level (TSH) because primary care doctors loved to say things like, *"We have a chance with patients in the hospital to check out some important values that might go missed in case they don't see a doctor for another ten years, like the TSH."* Or some similarly self-righteous line.

And Erica would suddenly lecture us all, smiling at the attending and chief, before reciting, "She's in the hospital, it's a chance to check out some important labs that might go missed in case she doesn't see a doctor for another ten years, like the TSH."

"Very good, Erica," complimented the attending.

Greg shook his head, fed up, and turned his chart notes over.

"Greg, finish your report," the chief ordered.

"I'm done."

Shelby, meanwhile, to avoid Erica's relentless pursuit of our mistakes, apologized before she even started her report. "I know I should have gotten a C-reactive protein level, and maybe an ultrasound, but I wanted to wait and see what labs her primary physician already had, so I'm sorry I don't have it all yet . . . I'm totally sorry."

Our average age was close to thirty and we were reduced to acting like remedial second graders.

Halfway through the month, the attending doctors rotated, and just to keep that elementary school feeling alive, we were given a mid-point evaluation. As with those elementary school evaluations (and I'm almost surprised our parents weren't invited to listen in as well), we sat down to be told our strengths and weaknesses. I squeezed into a chair short enough to have come right out of my elementary school classroom (no idea how it ended up in the conference room for me) and was promptly informed by the chief resident that she considered me a liability to both the hospital and our patients.

Excuse me?

She based her anything-but-constructive criticism on the fact that I fell asleep in rounds—which was true— but pointing out that it was Erica's fault would not help me. She then added that she was considering having me booted out of the residency program.

Say WHAT?

How could that critique not be scarring?

I wanted to point out that rounds were boring and that I thought she sucked as a chief resident. Instead, realizing I would merely look like the defensive eleven-year-old I felt, I sat quietly and decided I didn't like her. Not one bit. I was also a bit fearful that if I voiced what I was thinking, she would react instinctively like her *Officer and a Gentleman* counterpart and kick me in the groin, leaving me curled up in a ball, whimpering on the fourth floor.

I walked out of my evaluation upset with the entire system of medical training. My patients always received great care (at least in my opinion). There had never been a mistake with a single one of them (also my opinion). That pain-in-the-ass chief had even used my patient chart notes as an example of exemplary history and physical write-ups.

After walking around in a funk for several hours, wondering if I was about to be kicked out of medicine altogether, I discovered that both Shelby and Greg had also been accused of being "liabilities" to their patients, the hospital, and the residency program.

And then, to somehow make everything even worse, Erica, much to everyone's horror, was asked to start acting as the chief resident, assuming the leadership role she wantonly coveted on our team.

Good grief.

I hadn't even decided if I was going to continue residency the following year, but there was no way I was letting them kick me out. If I were going to screw up my life, it would be on my terms (Little did I know that I was only two months and one bike crash away from being placed on secret executive probation).

I decided I needed to change my ways for the better, really shape up—at least for the two remaining weeks on the service. I meditated on my current situation and my life goals. And I plotted an excellent and simple plan to remedy everything: For the next weeks I would tell my chief surgical resident girlfriend to stay away at night and I would drink coffee before rounds. Brilliant. There was no hanky-panky at night anyway, just a mixture of trying to sleep and pagers ringing. But coffee in the morning was the real kicker, as nobody in the hospital was prepared for me to show up awake and keenly focused.

I set the plan in motion and showed up nicely caffeinated for rounds. I made sure my notes were filled with every minute detail I could uncover on my patients. If Erica could take center stage and waste twenty minutes on her presentations, then so could I.

Instead of rushing through at my usual pace (the efficient version that everyone should follow so we could complete the rest of our morning work obligations), I took a deep breath and presented every intimate detail of my morning conversations with my patients: "Mrs. Tallybrand informed me that the baba ghanoush she ate last week has nothing to do with the chest pain and nausea she felt last night prior to admission and has promised us all the recipe if she can have extra Jell-o pudding. She's really lovely and I promised her the entire team would stop in to say hello after rounds." *Cue smile from attending for my art of medicine skills, combined with groans from all interns for wasting several precious minutes in their busy morning with that group patient visit.*

I took time to enunciate every single lab value ad nausea— including the previous day's lab levels for comparison.

When my arch enemy, the lame duck chief resident interrupted, bored with my presentation, and asked if I wanted to skip ahead to my radiology results instead of reviewing all the normal and unchanged lab results, I slowly looked up, shooting her a perturbed glance (best I could) and told her, "I'm getting there," looked down, and continued with my detailed lab values.

On my final evaluation, the new attending mentioned that she'd heard a rumor that I'd been slacking but thought I was doing a perfunctory job.

A year later, during my second year, I caught a glimpse of that same bitchy chief resident in a toy store (No, I wasn't shopping for myself) and just walked away—I never wanted to see her again lest I let fly words I would regret.

A few months after that evasive shopping maneuver, I discovered I could review the evaluations I had received on different rotations. I decided to take a look—and there, from that hellacious chief, was a lovely evaluation complimenting me as a hard-working resident that was highly valued on the team.

Huh?

I don't know what book of Machiavellian management she had misinterpreted—but I would not, as chief, emulate any of her methods. It was, however, nice to see that she had written a positive assessment of me. And I will admit, despite Erica driving all of us crazy, she is actually a very sweet person and truly wonderful doctor—but wow, did she drive me bananas that month.

FLASHBACK OVER
We now return to current day where it was my turn to be Chief.

SO NOW, YEARS LATER, I WAS IN CHARGE, AND MY RULES AND AGENDA were simple:

Be on time to morning report.

I would open the daily conference with something non-medical (a poem, a quotation), to help us ease into the day with inspired minds.

We would be efficient.

No intern would be forced to research answers to their own questions. I never liked when you were confused, already overworked, and asked a question seeking answers, only to be told, "That's a great question, why don't you bring us a report on it tomorrow."

And now I'll never ask a question again.

I would do the work of uncovering answers to their queries, as I did not want to stifle any desire to question appropriate medical care. We all knew the Family Practice service was miserable, with an abundance of work, notes, and documentation; along with social work coordination; but I wanted my chargé d'affaires to be as motivated as possible, learning, questioning, observing. Like inquisitive detectives we would dissect interesting cases and solve our patient's troubles as we zealously sharpened our skills of deduction throughout the hospital.

The team consisted of three interns, a mutinous second-year resident who would stage multiple coups in an attempt to wrest power from my hierarchical grasp, and five senior-year medical students doing sub-internships.

In addition to this motley band of future physicians we also had a pharmacy Ph.D. to highlight our oblivion regarding the drugs we prescribed; and of course, an attending physician to oversee my rule. The attending doctors were on board for two-week tours of duty, that being the duration to which they could tolerate our shenanigans.

Our attending physician for the first several weeks was fantastic. During one slap-happy morning rounds he shared a story from his residency, which remains one of my top-five foreign body stories:

Morning rounds that day had deteriorated into us not being able to stop laughing at the ludicrous reasons patients had been admitted overnight. Finally, unable to stop our giggling, the attending joined in, recounting some of his own horror stories from being a resident moonlighting in a small-town ER where he typically cared for car accident victims or patients with lacerations. One night however, a gentleman arrived with an apple lodged in his rectum. There was no way in the ER to remove this firmly placed fruit without tearing the patient's rectum—an undesired complication. So a surgeon was called in to help rectify the matter. The surgeon on call was a very proper doctor from India complete with thick accent; he decided that the best way to proceed was in the OR.

Beyond Monty Python skits for disarming somebody attacking you with a piece of fruit, there were very few resources for how to remove fruit from rectums, although chapters existed for how to remove other objects, so the OR was deemed the safest place to be for this trendsetting night. Everybody retreated to the OR, where the patient was placed, awake, on all fours on the operating table. The surgeon was able to delicately slice the apple and remove the pieces without cutting the patient's rectum.

As the surgeon walked out, he turned back, and with his thick Indian accent, deadpanned to the patient, "Next time, sir, you must chew your food." The patient almost fell off the table laughing along with the rest of the staff.

Halfway through the month the attending physicians swapped roles and we lost that great story-telling and genial teacher.

The second attending physician arrived to her first morning conference with my team and was shocked to find me acting as the chief. *She believed I was still an intern!* I had obviously made quite an impression on her as this remark came after she'd been one of my clinic bosses for two and half years. I was either somewhat invisible as a resident or had made absolutely no impact with her whatsoever. Or maybe she thought my medical skills were on par with being an intern? Either way, it was not a vote of confidence in front of the entire team.

———

MY VERY FIRST MORNING AS CHIEF, READY AND EXCITED, I BROUGHT juice and bagels to the team's morning report. We all assembled in our meeting room and before I had an opportunity to read my inspirational quotation for the day, my chief pager rang.

One of the most deflating moments for all the residents during the morning report was when the admitting chief's pager went off, thereby signifying that we were already being called to admit patients. It was a poor start to the day, having work loaded on before we'd even started the morning's standard chores. The call from the ER was for not one, but *two* possible patients to admit.

Patient admits equal more work. I nervously thought that this was a horrific omen. The residents would certainly see me as an albatross about their neck for the month, not a chief to be respected.

The ER patients were two young men who'd been found unconscious in their car, barely breathing. They had consumed some recreational party drugs, including GHB (the "date-rape" drug,) and one of them had passed out. The second patient was driving his unconscious friend to the hospital when he, too, proceeded to pass out, at a stop sign.

Fortunately somebody passing by noticed these barely-breathing party people slumped over in the car, which happened to be right across from the hospital. And that Good Samaritan, heroically recognizing the collapsed posture at a stop sign as being somewhat abnormal, dialed 911, thus saving both victims' lives.

The patients were rushed over to the ER where one of them was currently being intubated. GHB can lead to respiratory failure and the patients might have died without the assistance of the ER team providing respiratory support. The ER doctor explained what was happening and wanted to forewarn me in case they admitted either patient. I then told my future health care heroes what was happening downstairs.

One of the interns piped up, "Huh, I saw those guys passed out at that stop sign and figured they were just sleeping or something."

"Yeah, me too," said another intern.

So much for the Sherlock Holmes-like aspirations I had for my team.

Fortunately both young partiers recovered well in the ER and were sent home after being monitored without having to be admitted to our team. I breathed a huge sigh of relief having avoided that superstitious moniker of being an unlucky chief who attracted a high volume of patient admits.

As chief, I oversaw admitting all the patients, helped the residents, made sure the care was optimal for the patients, and kept the residents and interns working and learning. Despite that poor start to the first morning, everyone seemed to enjoy my plans for how to run the morning report.

My only problem child was the second-year resident who wanted to do things his way, questioning the care of everybody else's patients. I quickly remedied that problem by breaking my own rule and ordered him to give reports on any medical questions raised during morning report. He was then able to teach medicine to the team and was quite happy. In return I had less teaching to do and was also happy.

Early one Saturday, while my friends were out riding their bicycles and my resident team was seeing their patients, I snuck into the physician lounge, started reading the newspaper (oh man, I'm old), and eating a bagel. I was actually quite concerned that I would find nothing interesting to speed along my 24-hour hospital sentence. But lo and behold, just one bite into the bagel and "CODE BLUE" was called over the hospital PA.

If you thought running with scissors was dangerous, try running down a hallway in full stride, choking on un-chewed bagel with a stethoscope cracking the bejesus out of your kneecaps. Maybe I missed the class on how to run with a stethoscope, and maybe it was intuitive to fold it up or put it in your pocket, but for some reason (never wanting to relinquish my food perhaps?) I ran to a lot of codes with food in one hand, and the threshing like weapon of my stethoscope whipping around and smashing my patella. That was how, with bruised knees and close to requiring a bagel-dislodging Heimlich maneuver, I entered the ER where a young woman was in full arrest. Nobody knew why she was in cardiac arrest. She appeared young and otherwise healthy. We had no medical history to go on, no knowledge of what had triggered this situation.

I coughed up the bagel and immediately took over administering chest compressions.

We tried resuscitating her for quite some time, using a variety of treatments including cutting open an airway in her neck, injecting various drugs and performing CPR the entire time. I was dripping sweat giving chest compressions and was even complimented on my excellent technique. But all to no avail. We called the code twenty-five minutes later. Not the greatest way to start the day. Sometimes, fortunately a rarity, patients just did not survive. While I sat discussing the case with the ER doctor, I was told that there happened to be another ER patient waiting for me in room five.

The patient turned out to be a certain 315-pound, drooling, delusional schizophrenic that I had enjoyed the pleasure of admitting to the hospital multiple times over the last years. He'd spent the majority of his frequent hospital visits talking about the devil and asking for cigarettes. How fitting that I should get to admit him one more time.

The two of us had always had a somewhat confrontational relationship. Several months prior, we almost came to blows when I tried to convince him that smoking was a bad idea in general, and absolutely forbidden while he was in the ICU, intermittently requiring a ventilator for life-threatening pneumonia. But he eventually prevailed when, after being taken off the ventilator, an unsuspecting intern encouraged him to get up and walk around for exercise. So, he did. He walked right out of the ICU, straight out the front door of the building, and into a hospital courtyard where he lit up a cigarette. He passed out several minutes later in respiratory failure.

He was consequently re-intubated and put back on a ventilator. The ICU attending didn't find humor in the situation and made it as clear as you can be to a delusional schizophrenic with limited IQ, that if he wanted to kill himself, that was just fine—just go ahead and smoke outside again, and we wouldn't save him.

The unsuspecting intern who allowed the patient to get up and go walk around didn't get off much better.

A year earlier, the same exact patient had tried to convince me that evil spirits, a dragon, *and* the devil, "...are going to fly out of my [his] butt."

I tried to convince him that he needed to stay in the hospital to be treated for an abscess and that he should stop smoking. Neither one of us ever believed what the other one was trying to sell. However, when I finally saw the size of the abscess on his buttock, I began to believe something evil might indeed be let loose. So while he perceived my lectures on smoking cessation to be completely idiotic, I was starting to understand his concern with evil spirits flying out his backside—you judge who was winning.

And here he was on this fine Saturday with another big sore on his ass. My learning and experience over the last years became quickly evident. Instead of wasting hours arguing with him about smoking cessation and examining his otherwise unhealthy self, I walked in, looked at his swollen buttock, listened to his lungs, and left the room to get some supplies. Minutes later, the abscess was drained, and the patient was discharged. I was finally getting good at this doctoring business.

By the time we were senior residents, it was expected that we should be getting better at our chosen profession. The patient care started to feel somewhat routine—perhaps another sign that we were actually learning something. The cases that had once been challenging were now straightforward, and the hospital staff that once looked down on us, now treated us almost like peers in patient care, knowing our medical skills were not totally lacking.

Long ago the nurses might have called us for routine orders or questions, just to pester us as interns and to exhibit that they were higher in rank than us. Now, they often took on a protective role, only calling us if absolutely necessary and passing along important insights or concerns we might want to have ready to discuss with the attending physicians.

While the nurses, doctors and I started to recognize each other's true abilities, the patients had incorrectly assumed I knew what I was doing all along, but now, being both more efficient, and overseeing the team doing the real grunt work, I could not only round on all the patients very quickly, but also take time to appreciate the finer subtleties of what was happening medically, as well as admire the nonsensical conversations taking place every morning.

One such conversation was with Mrs. Wilde, a patient who the nurses had accused of recurrently falling out of bed during the night. It was mildly imperative to discover why, or if, she had actually fallen out of bed, as there was a consideration for tying her into bed with restraints, so she did not get up in the middle of the night, fall, and possibly break her hip. The restraints. however, had been known to accidentally strangle patients at a different hospital, so I was inclined to oppose their use if possible. After the nurse came and tattled to me about this falling down behavior, I went to question the patient about the incident:

"Mrs. Wilde, did you fall out of bed again last night?"

To which her hospital gown-wearing, 87-year-old roommate, wrestling with dementia, jumped in, "You can't get away with anything in this little town!"

While in the background Mr. Henry could be heard shouting from the neighboring room, "Let me out of this car!"

The previous night, Mr. Henry had announced to the nurse taking his vital signs, "Let's take our clothes off and start again!"

Hmm, to restrain or not to restrain, that remained the question.

"Mrs. Wilde, do you remember if you fell out of bed last night?"

"I don't think so. What do you think?"

"Don't listen to him, he thinks he's a doctor." Piped in the helpful roommate yet again.

At which point I left the room. Perhaps I felt nervous that a patient with dementia was seeing through my charade. Perhaps I realized the question-and-answer process was going nowhere. I opted to keep the patient out of restraints and requested the nurses monitor her more carefully. It was important to maintain your sanity.

As usual, an equally important concern was making sure that my team found time to re-fuel while marauding around the hospital for days at a time. Inevitably, during the short window that the cafeteria was open, another patient would code—there was some sort of Murphy's Law related to my hunger and codes being called. One Saturday evening, already peeved by the fact that I was spending an otherwise beautiful day indoors, I went to peruse the cafeteria's culinary blunders, when, on cue, a patient coded in the ICU.

My desire to appear dedicated to this patient's tenuous survival was not aided by my gastronomic concerns. While the patient was giving a heroic effort to move on to the next life, we tried using needle pokes and electric shocks to convince him of how much fun we were having here, and to please stick around. All the while I was wondering, how in the world my resident team (including myself) was going to eat now that we had missed the cafeteria's final meal.

Despite everyone's best efforts, the patient in arrest ultimately died. We stopped the code with everyone feeling a bit defeated. Patients in the ICU are typically quite sick, so it was possible that there was nothing else we could have done to revive this person. But it still felt like a bit of a failure.

Then, in a truly ridiculous moment, the respiratory therapist (who was in charge of the ventilator during the code), against orders, refused to extubate the patient after he was dead, stating that the family needed more time with him. In other words, she kept the ventilator going on a dead patient for an hour. I was famished, but the patient was dead and still breathing. I wasted my breath arguing with the therapist until I was finally able to contact the ICU attending to stop the madness.

Such moments demanded that I hand my credit card to an intern to go pick up some take-out food for dinner as I felt we deserved something to cheer us up—these were the truly important executive decisions I could now make to keep my team happy.

ALSO MEDICALLY OF INTEREST DURING NOVEMBER WAS MY OWN run-in with a small freckle on my chest. For no rational reason whatsoever, this tiny dark blemish bothered me. I found old photographs that showed no freckle where this tiny one now existed. I showed the freckle to several attending physicians in the program, all of whom said not to worry, give it a few more months and see what happens. This seemed like good solid advice from well-trained and established physicians.

I promptly went into an exam room and used a punch biopsy to cut the freckle out myself to send to the lab for examination.

A few days later the results returned and showed that the, *Oh, don't worry about it, it's fine,* freckle was one step away from malignant melanoma. I didn't really think too much of it until the powers that be in the residency program acted concerned. First, they acted concerned for my own mental well-being in dealing with this bad diagnosis.

Then a meeting was called to discuss my own rash decision to perform a procedure on myself. They were actually upset with me! *I* was the one who should have been upset with their faulty diagnostic skills. They should have been happy that I had saved their ass with my intuitive biopsy. All that mattered apparently was that I had once again managed to piss off the residency program, but still they didn't kick me out.

My month as Chief of the residents and sub-interns ended and I think my approach to being their Chief positively influenced everyone's consequent medical paths. My main message had been about following your heart in what was obviously a short time on this planet. And I think, despite everyone being busy, my point got through to them:

All three interns transferred to different residency specialties in order to follow their true medical desires—thereby infuriating the residency program.

All five medical students ranked our program number one for their residency matching—thereby pleasing the residency program.

As for me, well, word spread of my self-inflicted punch biopsy and somehow the rumors escalated. Several doctors became quite adamant that I never do another C-section on myself ever again.

The chief is dead, long live the chief!

OBSTETRICS

SEE A C-SECTION, DO A C-SECTION

As mentioned in the previous chapter, gossip regarding my self-inflicted punch biopsy rapidly spread, and no joke, chatter spiraled to the point that people believed I had performed complex surgery on myself. I suppose doctors don't have a lot to talk about beside medicine, but I was strictly prohibited from operating on myself again. Those warnings, however, did not apply to my operating on patients. Which was good, because I was back on the obstetrics ward, excited to assist with performing C-sections on my patients.

Did the enthusiasm run both ways? Doubtfully.

Our residency program had a weighty focus on Obstetrics, requiring that six months out of the three years be spent on OB services. We also had our own pregnant patients to see in our family practice clinic, which then required being the doctor for their child's delivery, and being the primary care doctor for mother and child afterwards.

To increase our training experience outside the smaller community hospital where family practice residents typically worked, we often rotated to the larger university hospital to train with specialty teams. The OB rotation at the University hospital was always a very busy service. During those loaded months at the university, OB patients from my clinic might also decide it was an opportune time to deliver their baby. These overlapping residency demands combined with unpredictable maternity schedules could lead to some long weeks.

On your night off from the OB wards, post-call, post-clinic, exhausted after a 36-hour shift and needing sleep, you might be called back to the labor and delivery deck at the community hospital to stay awake all night with an expectant mother that you had followed as a patient through her pregnancy.

Of course you wanted to be present for your own patients after getting to know them through their pregnancy. And since you made the effort to be there for the delivery on your night off, you were also expected to show up and see the postpartum and new baby patients early the next morning—which often led to interesting talks between exhausted mothers and language-restricted, fatigued doctors—and you had to be there *extra* early because you also had to report to a different hospital's labor and delivery deck (the university's in this case), where you were required to see patients quite early, as well.

My early morning discussions with Spanish-speaking patients were painful, even to my memory. My Spanish accent was decent enough that most patients incorrectly assumed I could speak Spanish, when in reality my medical vocabulary was quite limited. So I resorted to miming and making up words to the important questions we asked mothers after their delivery.

"Tienes un popo?" (*Have you pooped?*) I asked, pointing to my rear end and squatting up and down several times. Which would elicit confused comments from all family members present. That was my best effort to ask if the woman had gone to the bathroom.

"Estas como esto cuando cambiar?" (*Are you like this when you walk?*) I would ask as I spun my fingers around my head and staggered about the room. They never quite understood that charade until one day I finally asked a patient how to say "dizzy" in Spanish. And I won't even subject you to my embarrassing efforts (to everyone present) to asking how much vaginal bleeding was occurring.

Every time I brought up birth control, they appeared to think I was promoting mortal sins against the Church. Who was this crazed guy pointing at his ass, walking drunkenly across the room and trying to make us use contraceptives?

The mother, grandmother, aunt, sister and best friend would all start arguing in Spanish as I tried to pick out any word that I knew, "Blah blah blah comida blah blah domingo blah blah blah sangre."

Eat blood on Sunday? Are they requesting I perform a sacrifice? Or perhaps they are inviting me for Sunday dinner?

I would nod my head, smile, and say, "Gracias, pero, yo soy vegeteranio", while assuming that the OB medical student, who hopefully spoke more Spanish than me, would be in soon anyway to get the correct answers.

Despite linguistic stumbles, I felt I was in familiar territory on the labor and delivery decks. I believed I had quasi-mastered the system here—at least I knew where to find my patients. As before, there were the inevitable late-night nursery calls, deliveries at strange hours, deciding if women were in labor or merely uncomfortable with being pregnant and wishing they were in labor; but by now I was used to it all—accustomed to being sleep deprived, acquainted with the cafeteria salad bar, comfortable with the smell of amniotic fluid at 3 a.m., and all too familiar with spending the weekend in the hospital while my friends had play dates and sleepovers.

And at the same time, as mentioned, I was dealing with obstetric patients from my own clinic. There was a painful irony this month, the meaning of which eludes me beyond being a deity's whimsy, that on my nights off from the labor and delivery deck, when I was finally granted the chance to sleep and not stand between a woman's legs pulling out shrieking gremlins, I was *consistently* called back into one of the hospitals to deliver a clinic patient's baby.

While this proved to be an exhausting routine, the deliveries were with my own patients that I had come to know quite well over several months of their care. So being present for the actual delivery, once I was awake, after driving to the hospital in a pseudo-coma at 2 a.m., far outweighed missing the chance to see the completion of their pregnancy for some unnecessary sleep. I was in my thirties, my adrenals still functioned, and I had no kids of my own at home. There's no way I could handle those hours now.

One particular night I had gone out to dinner with friends, staying up to enjoy a glass of wine late into the evening. Passed out, exhausted, one of a few nights I was not on call, I heard a strangely familiar sound in my dream, a sound I knew all too well: the acrimonious cacophony of my arch-enemy belching its spurious tone—my pager.

Even through blurred vision I recognized the number of the University's labor and delivery floor—which meant that either I was dreaming, and they were calling to tell me that my Eastern European supermodel wife was delivering our baby, or back in reality, one of my clinic patients was delivering her own baby. I dressed and navigated the streets, which were somewhat hazy at that hour due to my eyelids straining to stay open, but still somewhat relishing the privilege of being woken up to share this pregnant woman's momentous event.

Privilege? I was obviously losing my mind.

Arriving on the university labor deck, I realized why I was almost enjoying this call to the hospital: I felt like a real doctor, showing up relaxed for the grand finale. Moreover, beyond being called in for the arrival of my patient's baby, I could still taste the sweetness of wine on my breath.

One of the staff's most favorite OB doctors was a mellow,

handsome guy whose patients all fell in love with him. When he swaggered onto the deck to deliver his patients late at night, there was always a whiff of wine about him—or perhaps he wore an Eau du Cabernet cologne? I never asked.

Wandering the hallways to the patient's room that night, I felt like that same OB doctor, showing up for a delivery with the faint trace of merlot hanging in the air.

The second reason that I, while fatigued, mostly didn't mind showing up for these deliveries was that typically the nurses called me in just in time for the delivery. Labor and Delivery nurses were tough when you were working, but once you'd been around for a while and had proven your own worth and dedication, they treated you like an actual doctor. On my off-call nights, they waited to page me until the woman was in the final stages of labor.

This night was different, however. I showed up to discover a woman not yet close to delivering, and certainly not resembling my imaginary Eastern European supermodel wife—an Eastern European weightlifter, perhaps. She was propped on pillows, moaning and crying loudly for an epidural, which, at this point of the night, with her agonizing yells bouncing around my skull, I was all too happy to order for us both. Oftentimes, once a woman in labor had an epidural placed, she relaxed, and the labor progressed more rapidly. Tonight we experienced the opposite effect.

The epidural was placed, the patient relaxed, and the force of her contractions not only weakened, they also became far less frequent. When I had initially walked in the door to her shouts of pain, we all thought she must be mere minutes away from delivering.

Now, for several contractions after the epidural, the nurse, husband, and I maintained the optimism that the baby was indeed about to arrive. We shouted encouragement with each push and contraction, waiting excitedly in sweaty gown and gloves for the newborn's appearance.

Thirty minutes later the top of the tyke's head had not descended any further, and our enthusiasm waned. The husband turned on the room's television and started flipping channels. At first, I thought it a bit callous to watch TV instead of staring at his wife not delivering their child. Then, over the next hour, all our concentration slowly turned from the woman in labor, and the baby's teasing tuft of hair, to the television shows playing above the bed.

The husband, nurse, and I would be startled back from staring, mesmerized by the late-night television's glowing pull, to the pregnant woman calling, "Excuse me, I think I'm having a contraction."

We would turn around, glance at the monitor and pull our attention away from whatever show was playing to get through her now useless pushing efforts, and quickly return attention to the episode in progress. Amazing how engrossing late-night television can be. We all became completely engrossed, despite the pregnant woman's selfish attempts to have us watch her non-progressing labor. "Hey, I'm having another contraction over here."

Shhh, we're watching the show, call us if anything happens this time, was what I wanted to say. But instead we smiled and tried to help her through her labor. At one point, the idea of a C-section was mentioned, a suggestion that frequently caused pregnant women to push even harder to force their labor to progress. And, eventually with the sun starting to rise, and my sleep now forgotten, she finally delivered a healthy child. No C-section.

And I didn't have to drive to work, I was already there. What a blessing.

DAYS LATER, I WAS ONCE AGAIN CALLED TO THE HOSPITAL IN THE middle of the night for one of my own clinic patients. The OB nurses had been carefully monitoring her and now, close to 1 a.m., they decided she might need a C-section. Out of respect to her doctor (that's me), they had called me to come in for the delivery, *and* to ask if I agreed with their assessment.

I looked over the patient's notes, contraction tracings, and baby heart rate tracings to evaluate their decision...

Who am I kidding? Of course I agreed. The labor and delivery nurses were OB experts and knew exactly what was needed. But she was my patient, an eighteen-year-old girl with her first pregnancy.

I had embarrassed myself with this patient several times. The first time I had done a physical exam that includes a pelvic exam, she warned me that she had just had a Brazilian wax job because it might make the delivery cleaner. No idea how one responds appropriately to such statements. I fumbled through a slew of incomprehensible comments and decided to just shut up and do the exam.

Then, months later, as she approached full term, she called my cell phone with a question about her possibly being in labor (I thought I was quite the hip doctor, giving my cell phone number out to my OB patients—never again did I make such a mistake). We talked through her concerns about the pain, and I thought she was more likely experiencing Braxton-Hicks contractions (which can be extremely painful and similar to real labor contractions— don't believe the books that say they are not severe!), causing her discomfort. We agreed that she was not yet in real labor and seemed well enough to stay at home. "I'll see you next week for your weekly visit, but call or get back in sooner for anything concerning, like we discussed, OK?"

"OK, thanks Dr. Lawrence, Bye."

"Bye. Love you."

Dead silence.

I quickly hung up.

EXCUSE ME? WHAT? "LOVE YOU????"

The words had reflexively fallen from my mouth as if I was

saying goodbye to my mother, grandmother, or non-existent girl-friend. I was mortified. Totally tired, automated mistake and I had no inkling of whether I needed to call a hospital lawyer to see if I was about to be brought up on charges unbecoming a physician.

Instead, I sweated our next appointment, not sure if it would be worse to find out she had swapped doctors, or if she showed up and asked me, point blank, what was wrong with me. *Fatigue and reflexive phone manners, I swear!*

But we had survived my silly blunders, and there we were, middle of the night, her labor not progressing. I walked into her room and explained that with the current situation, we all thought it best if she had a C-section.

"You want to do a C-section?"

"We think it's best. You've been in labor for a long, long time, and even with the medicine helping your contractions, the baby's not any closer to delivering, and you're wearing out. So, yes, I think it's best. Are you OK with it?"

"Are you going to be there?

"Yes, of course."

"Then OK."

And very soon thereafter we were in the Operating Room, patient, nurse, OB attending, anesthesiologist, and me. My patient's abdomen was prepped (cleaned for surgery), and we were ready to start.

I could assist a C-section in the dark. Years later, my wife's OB, who knew me from my time in school and residency, offered to let me assist on my wife's C-sections so that I could bill for the procedure (I stayed next to my wife, not operating).

I stood, ready to assist, waiting for the OB attending to draw the ink marks over the landmarks on the patient's abdomen where he would make the incision into her belly. But then he looked over at me and said, "I've seen you. You know what you're doing."

And he handed me the surgical marker.

What???

Cue excited gasp from audience.

This was really, really exciting. But I acted cool and collected:

I marked my patient's abdomen, opened my hand to receive the scalpel, and made the first incision through her skin along her bikini line. The attending doctor used the Bovie instrument to cauterize any points of bleeding, assisting *me* in performing the actual procedure. This was awesome.

I made further incisions, inserted retractors to protect the bladder... and everything went perfectly. I carefully handed off a perfectly healthy baby girl to the nurse and repaired the surgery: massage uterus; suture it back together; suture abdomen back together, staple skin on abdomen closed.

I finished writing orders for the mother and baby around 2:30 a.m. I was due back in a different hospital in a few hours but would need to check on these two patients first. The attending nodded at me. "Good job in there, you should consider an OB fellowship."

The rare moments you were recognized as competent in someone else's specialty were very nice, all the more so since my own residency program was looking for reasons to kick me out. But at that time, I was just doing the required job and didn't think twice about it.

I had actually thought about pursuing OB—but the reality of living the crazy hours for years, not weeks, was a bit intimidating. I smiled my appreciation. And then the senior OB resident on-call made me even happier:

"Don't worry about rounding on her in a few hours, we have it covered. Thanks for coming in, heard you did a nice job."

I was being treated like a real doctor at the big university hospital. Again, you might be thinking this was all normal and natural after years of training. But you have to understand that in most moments, you are just working non-stop and don't really have time to reflect (until right now, writing this book many years later), and to recognize, retrospectively, the small moments of validation where you started to very sub-consciously think, and therefore act, like you knew what you were doing and could actually become a doctor. And in general, compliments are *very* rare. Everyone just worked hard. Exemplary care was the expectation, not something deserving praise.

That said, I think the University OB team, tough though it might've been compared to our smaller community hospital with a friendly, tight-knit OB team, actually accepted me for working hard. As a resident, I'd done a good job and worked some notoriously crummy shifts, like most holidays, including being on call on January 1, 2000.

FLASHBACK INTERN YEAR

DECEMBER 31, 1999, THE THOUSAND-YEAR WAIT FOR THE TURN OF the millennium was upon us and I needed to arrive at my new service, High-Risk Obstetrics at the University Hospital, at 5 a.m. on January 1, 2000, the morning after *the* New Year's Eve party we had waited a lifetime to enjoy. I'd been assigned this enviable schedule, which included being on-call through the night, because I was not only an intern, but also a family practice intern, i.e. not an OB/GYN intern.

OB at the University hospital involved a lot of high-risk deliveries, and the OB residents were appropriately quite demanding. Showing up hungover, or still drunk, would likely require I be flogged, shrugged off as an idiot, possibly dismissed, and certainly not likely to be trusted with any deliveries. The OB residents worked hard all the time, and we family practice residents were expected to do our best to keep up. The expectations were actually fine by me; I liked working on the OB services.

And the beautiful part of being a resident on this particular University Hospital service was that they always had a full team of medical students working. And I was actually higher on the totem pole than the medical students—the hierarchy was finally, however slightly, tilting in my favor.

As a medical student, I'd been required to visit all the post-partum patients (mothers who had recently delivered), write all their notes before morning rounds, and present them to the entire team. Then an intern would sign off on our notes. But now *I* was the intern, and merely had to visit the patients before scribbling my initials on the medical student's notes.

Since the tedious note writing aspect was taken care of by the students, I could spend more time talking with the patients; I could pass on my sage years of wisdom to the medical students; I could even sleep an extra ten minutes knowing the students were already hard at work seeing our patients. This was beautiful.

Unfortunately, on Saturday, January 1st, 2000, AD, the medical students were still drunk and dancing on holiday and had not yet started their rotations.

I therefore returned to my regularly scheduled position, squatting down at the bottom of the totem pole, and started the millennium by asking new mothers if they had passed gas, had a bowel movement, or felt dizzy. How fitting.

So I woke up around 4:20 a.m. on January 1, 2000, discovered that all the lights and computers still worked despite the Y2K fears, and headed into the hospital. I worked all day, stayed up all night, and saw OB patients the next day, Sunday, January 2, 2000. That was how I enjoyed my first weekend of the new century. For me, partying like it's 1999 means missing parties, going to bed early, and working a thirty-two-hour shift. Fuck you Prince and your stupid *1999* song. (I actually really like Prince's music).

That intern month on high-risk OB turned out to be quite valuable educationally, as the residents took time to teach me, and in turn, I took time to teach the medical students—I was not too far removed from remembering how confusing it was to learn how to present patients at morning report; how to measure cervical dilation; how to deliver a baby; or how to ask a foreign- speaking patient what form of birth control they would like to use after delivering their baby.

FLASHBACK OVER

AS MENTIONED, ONE EXCELLENT EDUCATIONAL ADVANTAGE (I'M being sarcastic) of being a family practice resident was that while the OB residents went home post-call; we few, we special few, had the additional learning opportunity of seeing our clinic patients without having slept in 33 hours. Sound healthy for me or the patients? No, no it wasn't. At that point I believe I responded to patients with grunts, as it was often all I could muster as I tried keeping my eyes open—but at least my family practice *art of medicine* instructors, the ones teaching us to make encouraging noises to let the patients know we were interested in what they were saying, would be happy.

We were instructed that caring for OB patients in the clinic was true family practice medicine. We would care for the mother before, during and after delivery, and then become the newborn's pediatrician as well. It was supposed to be quite rewarding, and yet my clinic patients never seemed to fit into the normal, typical, or rewarding categories.

One of my most perplexing and frustrating set of clinic patients was a wonderful refugee family, newly arrived in Salt Lake City from Sudan. Our first encounter was for the woman's initial OB visit. OB visits were usually straightforward, especially if the woman spoke English.

Initial OB visits required a lot of history-taking about a woman's physical health, pregnancy history, and ordering a small battery of lab tests. Follow-up OB visits, until a woman is close to delivery, are simply checking urine samples for signs of sugar or hypertension, and measuring "fundal height."

Fundal height, a measurement of how big the uterus is growing, is one of nature's craziest cocktail party tricks. Imagine this, somehow, the measurement from an expectant mother's pubic symphysis bone to the top of the fundus (the uterus), when healthy and measured in centimeters, was the same as the number of weeks a woman was pregnant! Come on, that's a pretty cool parlor trick you can use the next time you're in a bar flirting with an unknown pregnant woman and want to impress her by guessing how far along she is.

OK, I admit, that sounds like an unlikely event, but it's still a pretty cool measurement and certainly serendipitous evidence that we should all move to the metric system.

Beyond party tricks, it's a useful and quick measurement to judge if a woman's uterus is growing appropriately, or at all. If not, it's cause for concern and time to check for what could be causing the lack of growth.

Back to the clinic where I first met this Sudanese family, all of us completely unaware of how much time we would eventually share together. She was a tall, elegant woman sitting straight-backed and silent. Her husband, a strapping young Djimon Hounsou doppelganger, immediately took over the conversation for his wife, who did not appear to speak English.

For many months, I listened to her husband translate and tell me about her problems, which were many and very elusive. He told me of vague pains in her rectum and her vagina—which I never quite figured out. Vague problems with her skin being dry, which had something to do with stomach pain—never figured those out. Vague knee problems, which were never present during our visits—and no, I never figured that problem out either.

I ordered one test after another to determine why she had this terrible and vague stomach/vaginal/rectal/knee pain with dry skin. I read books looking for answers. I wrote a variety of prescriptions, hoping one of them would help with her problems —problems that only appeared to exist somewhere in the looking glass with Alice.

Nothing ever turned out to be wrong with her—in fact she looked amazing; she glowed with pregnancy. Heads turned and stared when this gorgeous, strikingly elegant couple walked into the clinic. But her husband complained through every one of our visits, shaking his head about how terribly everything was going. There were definite moments, when, in a post-call haze, exhausted, I wanted to tell them to go find a wiser doctor than me, one who might solve their myriad of mysteries, because I was obviously an idiot.

Finally, when I was on my obstetrics rotation at the more erudite University Hospital and discussed this perplexing case, an OB resident suggested that I consider the woman might be depressed. She had been transplanted from home; away from any family; had experienced violent trauma fleeing as a refugee; survived a life of poverty, etc. Okay, put it that way, it made sense that depression might enter the picture, and the many vague, intermittent symptoms she was experiencing would fit with a diagnosis of depression.

We were accustomed to depression in our culture, but not so in other cultures where depression might play out in more physical or visceral experiences as there was no normal way to describe or communicate those feelings. I finally felt confident that I had the correct answer to bring to our weekly meeting, I could finally address and help her. I was almost giddy with having solved the mystery, and empathically wanted them to finally feel safe and welcome in their new home where caring people were treating them.

We sat down in our next clinic meeting, and I tried to discuss depression with them.

I received blank stares.

When asked about the possibility of mental stress, her husband flatly denied this as an option—which I do not think he actually understood, this cultural difference being at the heart of what I was suggesting, at least in my very own made-up mind.

But no, depression was apparently not an option to this family. I'm not sure if they appeared more disappointed in my constantly failing diagnostic abilities, or if I was simply deflated for not having solved all their problems in one fell swoop.

And then one day, months later, when the husband was unable to attend our scheduled meeting for the first time, and his wife was alone for our visit, I experienced an amazing revelation. Initially I was totally apprehensive of how we would now communicate without her husband translating for us, and I was somewhat nervous about making some cultural mistake in what I might ask her without her husband present.

Then she started talking to me.

And not just talking—but talking in English.

She spoke English?

Yes, she spoke English! She not only spoke English, but it turned out she spoke it quite well, far better than her husband. I was shocked. She lucidly explained her problems and what was bothering her—which was nothing too abnormal for a pregnant woman, just discussing what she felt, physically and emotionally. She reassured me that she was not very concerned as this was her second pregnancy, the first having gone very well.

Rather than give any proper medical response, I kept jabbering away about how shocked I was that she spoke English so well.

She smiled gracefully at my blabbering.

During all subsequent visits, with her husband present, she sat quietly, while we two males hacked apart years of spoken languages into misunderstood facial gestures, shrugs and bobbing head motions. But at least I now knew she was healthy and doing well—and months later I helped her deliver a healthy baby boy.

OUTPATIENT PEDIATRICS

THE FIERCELY COMPETITIVE WORLD OF
MEDICAL SPORTING EVENTS

I was blessed with shadowing a pediatric doctor in her clinic office for my required, and overdue, outpatient pediatric rotation. *Blessed?* Yes, indeed, a non-call month (i.e. weekends off and no nights in the hospital) was enough to make me giddy in my skivvies—and the pediatrician I requested to work with occasionally limited her schedule to working half-days!

Scheduling electives was similar to registering for college classes where students quickly shared beta about which professor's classes to sign up for and which ones to avoid at all costs. We residents picked up rumors of which physicians were excellent teachers, which ones worked easier schedules, which let you go home earlier in the day, and which expected you to work full weekends along with handing in written assignments.

Working this pediatric rotation confirmed my previous statements that pediatricians are trained to treat the parents of sick kids. The kids, in most cases, seemed to get better. The parents, however, were likely to remain anxiously concerned about their children for eternity. During that month we saw many little patients with ear infections, bad colds, and worse tempers. We treated these sick children with antibiotics or cold medicine, and their parents with affirmations and reassurances. Far more entertaining than treating pediatric coughs and sniffles, however, were the annual Well-Child Checkups (WCC).

I am convinced that children's annual Well-Child Checkups provide some of the most competitive playing fields in medicine today—a yet-to-be monetized sporting arena not suitable for parents weak of heart or spirit.

The WCC games kicked off by documenting for the entire world, and *especially* the parent's competitive friends with children of their own, to see for all time, their child's ability to grow, gain weight, and increase their head circumference. I was initially taken aback watching parents aggressively fist-pumping when informed that their toddler hit the 90% mark in any category. I was all the more agog witnessing parents shamefully turning away, heads hung low to hide repressed tears upon hearing below national average scores—as if their child's now infamously average head circumference was a result of their time partying a bit too hard back in university.

Next up, it was time for the biggest event of the day: developmental milestones. Developmental milestones were designed to drive parents absolutely batshit bananas.

The way certain parents gasped, "Thank God," upon hearing that their child was using toys appropriately for his age, made me envision them in bed the night before, sleeplessly fretting whether their precocious baby JoJo was going to stack blocks correctly. I don't think it farfetched to guess that some parents actually hired tutors for the stressful block-stacking challenge.

And what's with stacking blocks being used to measure kid's development? Was there some primordial brain function, a fight or flight survival response to a circling pack of hyenas that made advanced cave-kids think, *must stack rocks quick*. And those that stacked the best protective barriers survived to become our ancestors?

And then, just today, as I sit editing, a headline pops up from Georgetown University, my alma mater, that an article in *Developmental Psychology* written by a Georgetown graduate, shows the association between stacking blocks (requiring fine motor skills and a willingness to investigate environment) at an early age, and predicting advanced reasoning at adolescent stages. That's just a crazy coincidence because I have never ever in my life seen another article about stacking blocks. In fact, I am dismissing the whole thing and considering this the power of manifestation or possibly proof we live in a simulation.

The stressful stacking blocks event will be center stage if my idea to put the WCC sporting event on TV comes to fruition. But there were no lack of other high-pressure games to keep parent's on edge: Hand-wringing, encouraging smiles, and gentle suggestions to help wee Kenzie spell her name (part of the WCC routine).

Eye rolls and disbelief that young master Henry had less than fifteen words in his vocabulary.

Parental high-fives when the doctor witnessed chubby infant Frederick rolling over by himself.

To be fair, now that my wife and I have our own three children, I realize all parents of infants and toddlers are sleep-deprived, spend their days interacting with people of limited vocabularies, have heightened emotions, and should not be judged by their behavior.

The underlying concern seemed to be that those infants running behind in their milestones were slated to work menial labor jobs in Siberia. Nobody had ever proven that if Little Baby Billy couldn't stack three blocks before his second birthday that he was destined to shovel horse manure. Nor have studies confirmed that toddlers rolling over at three months are destined to win Nobel Prizes.

I would not be surprised, however, if the crazy Swedes, ever enthusiastic for more medical studies, were doing research on what happened to twins, Olaf and Sven, if their parents were told Sven was a moron because he only had five words in his vocabulary when he was supposed to have seven; and that Olaf was the second coming because he crawled three hours earlier than expected.

Would Sven be nurtured as much as Olaf? Would he be shunned and denied his Yak milk? Would he slowly accept his destiny as the disgruntled Zamboni driver at the local rink while brother Olaf became the town's leading scorer on and off the ice? We wait with bated breath for news from Sweden.

And just in case you're wondering, I walked at seven months —*way* ahead of schedule. Just thought you should know. I also brought my highchair down on my own head several days later, requiring sutures in my forehead, and getting an early start on my head injuries.

I have also worked shoveling horse manure.

I have never driven a Zamboni (yet).

I FURTHERED MY PEDIATRIC KNOWLEDGE WORKING WITH A HIGHLY-touted pediatric dermatologist. Dermatologists have a very nice life. First off, the hours are good—there are very few dermatologic emergencies that require a late-night presence in the hospital. Second, they're paid well. Third, there was no shortage of patients. It is also one of the most competitive residency fields—i.e., only really smart people become dermatologists.

Dermatologists might have a bad rap for getting paid big money to pop zits, dole out acne medicine, and remove unsightly moles—but they are also responsible for tracking deadly skin cancer (a concern of my own after my self-inflicted chest punch biopsy).

While skin cancer may be a rarity in the pediatric age group, any parent will tell you that a skin rash on their child is quite concerning; and if you managed to subdue a teenager's acne, parents and patients loved you forever.

The fourth beautiful aspect of dermatology was that you either cut things off or, more commonly, prescribed either steroid cream or antibiotics to see if the rash went away—that was it. You could diagnose acne and prescribe appropriate medicines, or make a few hundred other diagnoses that were all treated the same way: start the patient on either steroids or antibiotics, and then see what happens. And for the really bad cases, I learned to prescribe steroids *and* antibiotics, and then have them follow up in several weeks to, you guessed it, see what happens.

My role here was the same as in every other rotation: go see patients, learn about their ailment, examine whatever needed examining, and then go tell the doctor about it. With dermatology, I would ask the young patients what kind of rash they had and how long it had been around, look at it, usually be afraid to touch it, and then describe it to – you guessed it – the doctor.

Dermatologists, like all other doctors, had their own special vocabulary. If you could describe what the rash looked like properly, knew the timeframe of its appearance and its location on the body, you could usually narrow down the differential diagnosis (the list of likely diagnoses) quite accurately.

On other medical services outside of dermatology, there were only a few words in our medical jargon needed to describe a rash. On those clinical rotations, 99% of rashes were described as "red." If you wanted to appear really gung-ho in describing a rash, you might add that it was "macular/papular" or "vesicular." Whether it was or wasn't, using those words made it appear that you had actually looked at the rash and taken time to document it in your report.

But on the dermatology service you were expected to expand your dermatologic vocabulary and complete the rotation with an ability to describe skin lesions using words beyond "red" and "macular/papular."

After my time on that service, I was proud to say I'd expanded my vocabulary to include at least five or six new words I could freely use to describe a pediatric rash. Regardless, they all got better with steroids or antibiotics.

PEDIATRIC PATIENTS IN MY OWN CLINIC WERE ALSO FUN BECAUSE, AS I've pointed out, the kids usually got better no matter how I tried to interfere with their wellbeing. The scary part was that you did not want to miss the one strange, or dangerous, diagnosis by assuming everything would just resolve naturally. Pediatric medicine, as mentioned, mostly seemed to revolve around treating the parents' anxiety about their child, along with my own anxiety about missing a diagnosis, while the kids got better.

The same Sudanese family who came to see me regularly for OB visits (see previous chapter) would occasionally show up with the whole family for one of their appointments. The father, the same one who complained about his healthy wife's vague pains, had suddenly decided he needed to complain about each of his healthy children's imaginary problems as well.

During one such visit, this father's biggest concerns was that their 18-month-old son had "bad legs." He explained to me that the child was always falling over and not walking well. As the father communicated his anxiety about his son's legs, I watched this supposed 18-month-old invalid running laps around the room and vaulting effortlessly over the exam table. I looked up incredulously at the dad with a questioning glance; he then told me it was much worse when his son wore shoes.

I examined the boy's legs—they seemed normal in every aspect. We put on his shoes and the kid ran an 11-second 100-meter dash down the hallway. But the father was still convinced, shaking his head, "He has bad legs."

I didn't know what to do.

I fell back on recommending a "follow-up." That was the beauty of clinic visits, you could ask people to schedule a follow-up visit. Hopefully, by the time of their next appointment, everything had improved, and they would cancel their visit last minute, thus leaving a free moment on your schedule to catch up with paperwork. They didn't teach that brilliant piece of time management in *The Art of Medicine* class!

When the *"Come back for follow-up"* approach didn't work, however—when they came back with the same complaint—it was a complete backfire: you'd been unsure of a diagnosis in the first place and now what could you do? Order labs, X-rays, or transfer their care to a more intelligent specialist.

And eventually you accepted you could not heal everyone. But you *wanted* to fix everybody, you believed that was your role—and those frustrating emotions stuck with me through my entire medical career. Some patients were fatigued for reasons you would never uncover nor fix and thankfully, most pediatric patients, regardless of what you did, got better.

But not this young man with *bad legs*. I saw that kid almost every week for months and he seemed totally fine: he ran; he jumped; he skipped; he danced the Watusi; he vaulted tall furniture with enviable skill for anyone twice his age. I wanted to alert a sports agent friend to buy stock in this tyke.

But the father was convinced: "Bad legs."

I avoided doing any unnecessary X-rays but did eventually send them for a pediatric orthopedic consult—who also found nothing abnormal.

Sorry to say, I never found anything to help solve that kid's mysteriously bad legs. In truth, the far greater mystery was why this family, who by now had routinely experienced my complete inability to do anything about any of their multiple enigmatic problems, returned week after week to see me, the apparently useless clinic simpleton?

I don't know.

But when parents bring kids to your clinic, you do everything you can to help. You scour books (now google—yes, we frequently *google*) to figure out what could be wrong with the patient, and all the more so with kids.

Ear infections are one common reason parents bring their children to the doctor. Most of the infections are viruses. This means that prescribing antibiotics will do nothing to fix the infection, but will likely give the kid diarrhea, while the infection healed itself over time. But giving antibiotics makes the parents and the doctor feel like they're doing something helpful, like boosting the economy with increased diaper and baby wipes sales.

I could probably tell parents to take their kids home, dress them in lederhosen, yodel into the bad ear twice a day, and the kid would get better almost as frequently as they improved on antibiotics. While yodeling therapy might potentially lead to hearing loss, along with an unexpected appreciation for oompah music, the antibiotic regimen was not much better regarding incurred adverse effects: diarrhea and battling the kid two or three times every day to funnel medicine down their unappreciative, gagging throats, for example.

There was even another one of those pesky Scandinavian studies proving that over 90% of children got better without treating their ear infections with antibiotics. But try telling a parent who had not slept in two nights, and had just paid an expensive co-pay, whose child was crying and not eating because they felt miserable with a fever, that Scandinavian people didn't use drugs because of a study, so you weren't going to prescribe their kid drugs either.

As the parents stared at you, no doubt thinking that the M.D. behind your name stood for "Medical Disaster," and that maybe you needed a slap about the head, you piped up defensively, "Look at all those Swedish bikini models, their ears look fine, and they never had antibiotics." The parent would promptly look for another physician who thought the Swedes should stick to taking saunas and building Volvos.

A quick question, what is up with the Scandinavians and their research? I imagine this conversation:

"Hey, Rolf, let's go ski cross-country!"

"Uff-da, Tomas, I am out of muesli and need some cash, so I am going to sign up for some medical experiments."

Maybe that's not exactly how it works, but there is an awful lot of research coming out of those Nordic countries, and most of it seems to say Western medicine has been doing some silly things that are complete bunk, medically, and merely benefit pharmaceutical company profits.

Hopefully you realize I am being flippant and agree there are plenty of times that antibiotics are the proper treatment for an ear infection—but how to decide? You must look and assess the infection using your doctor skills. Some infections should be immediately treated with antibiotics, and some should not, and most fall in-between, meaning you can watch to see how they change over the next days. But what parent wants to wait several days to treat a screaming kid by returning to their doctors office? Not many I met over the subsequent years. And doctors also feel that parental pressure to treat sick kids with medicines.

I do believe parents know their kids best, have learned what works for them and should be listened to when they say their children are sick. It creates a tough balance for doctors who want to provide appropriate treatment, but also feel real pressure from parents that might conflict with their own assessment—choices made all the more difficult as not every decision is absolutely clear.

Beyond the need to please parents who have paid their expensive co-pay, there is also the legal aspect of medical decision-making. If I document that an infant has an ear infection, and I then convince the parent not to treat the infection with antibiotics because it looks very mild and is likely viral, there is a good chance everything will be fine.

If, however, their precious pooping machine ruptures an eardrum from the infection, and one day the child is diagnosed with mild hearing loss, they will likely blame me, and consider legal action for my stingy doling of drugs. So we cover our ass and write a prescription for most infections. I'm quite sure the legal reality check was also not in the art of medicine lectures.

My typical way to treat more moderate or mild ear infections, when the eardrum was slightly red, but without pus or fluid or pressure building in the ear, was to recommend watching it for a few days and treating the child with medicine to relieve the pain as necessary (ibuprofen or Tylenol), and if things worsened, i.e. fevers were higher or the pain not controlled, to then start the antibiotics, or preferably, return to the clinic so I could re-examine the patient.

And on the topic of over-prescribing antibiotics: This whole medicine game was just not as perfect as people supposed.

Sorry out there, but it's true, the overuse of antibiotics with known risks and proliferating bacteria resistance to drugs was pretty common knowledge and considered poor doctoring. But it happened, anyway. Ask any doctor about the amount of Zithromax, an easy-to-take five-day antibiotic treatment, purchased annually to treat what are likely viral chest colds, or bronchitis (which is inflammation, and not an infection)—it probably exceeds the GNP of Latvia. Bad medicine? Often cover-your-ass medicine, or placate-patient medicine, but, in fact, some doctors knowingly did bad things just to make their job easier (*cue horrified gasp!*).

One ER physician working in an Urgent Care clinic I managed years later proved the point. A nurse pulled me aside and told me that this doctor had been drawing positive lines with a blue pen on the rapid-strep tests—which made his caring for the patients pretty easy, as he could quickly write a prescription and send patients out the door satisfied with his rapid care and thinking they would be better in two days.

When one of the nurses saw him do it repeatedly, he claimed to be playing a practical joke on another nurse. Those patients, or parents of patients, however, left with unnecessary, and possibly harmful prescriptions for themselves or their kids.

That doctor claimed he never did anything of the sort.

Unfortunately that was not his only downfall and despite being a respected ER doctor—got the boot from yours truly. He was mad as hell to be fired by a young doctor lacking his years of experience. A year later he was in trouble with a whole lot of people experienced in law enforcement for prescribing an over-abundance of pain medications.

Fortunately he was the exception. The vast majority of doctors I have known, as in over 99%, go out of their way to provide the best possible care for their patients. And while I'm pointing out exceptions, as much as I've made some glib (albeit accurate) comments about pharmaceutical companies, they, too, do amazing work to design and test life-saving medications—we all just needed to use them responsibly.

And if you think antibiotics are not really that dangerous, go read the Burn Unit chapter in *PLAYING DOCTOR; PART ONE* to learn about an otherwise healthy girl who took a common antibiotic for a viral head cold. After lying unconscious and intubated in the ICU for months with her skin peeling off from a severe toxic reaction to the drug, she then required a bilateral lung transplant. Made me forever very wary of prescribing unnecessary antibiotics.

SNOWBIRD SKI RESORT CLINIC/PHONE CALL DUTY

I MISS MY CALLING AS A STEAMY MEDICAL NOVELIST

The Sundance Film Festival was in town. And since I dreamed of making movies, I thought it best to attend the festival as much as possible—which, as a medical resident, was not too frequently. Fortunately, my spirits were lifted as I was also spending the month working as the greatly envied medical resident at the Snowbird Ski Resort Clinic.

Similar to my work at the Telluride Mountain Clinic during medical school, we treated victims brought off the ski hill with injured knees, strained necks, lacerations, head colds, or feeling sick due to the high altitude.

Our job at the clinic was to either make them better or, if unable to treat them adequately, send them to hospital. The nurses at the Snowbird clinic, many of them ER nurses, could evaluate and treat many of the cases without really needing any doctors butting in to complicate things. They were great teachers and invited me onto the team with open arms.

Despite the nurses' level of expertise, the doctors were legally required to sign off on all the cases, and to perform most of the procedures, like suturing up the lacerations, or reducing dislocated shoulders (putting them back in place). I had received wonderful tutelage at the Telluride clinic for treating dislocated shoulders. In fact, the simple technique I had been taught worked so well that I had helped put people's shoulder's back in joint in the middle of ski runs, on beaches, in parking lots, and it worked easily and every time. So, when an injured skier crashed into our care with a dislocated shoulder, I figured we would follow that simple procedure and move on. Instead, multiple attending doctors were present that day (typically there was only one head doctor staffing the clinic), and they all wanted to show-off *their* favorite technique for putting shoulders back in place.

The patient, moaning in pain, was moved off the ski patrol stretcher onto a clinic bed, and taken for an X-ray which confirmed his shoulder was dislocated. Then the first doctor assured the patient he would be feeling better as soon as he (the doctor) fixed the problem with his guaranteed to work every time shoulder reduction technique.

First, the doctor tried rotating and moving the shoulder into its socket—a textbook procedure. The patient yelled because he was in pain, which made him tense up, causing the muscles to go into worse spasm, which makes reducing it more difficult. So, the other doctor recommended administering some pain meds and muscle relaxants to help the patient relax.

The doctors tried again with the same result: patient screaming with his shoulder still dislocated.

They tried wrapping a towel around the patient's body and pulling him one way while his arm was yanked the other direction. Nothing doing. More pain, increased muscle spasm, and doctors sweating from effort.

They tried hanging a weight off the bed to pull the shoulder into place. Nothing.

One of these doctors was an orthopedic surgeon and the other was a sports medicine trained doctor, i.e. they both knew what they were doing. So I, the useless observing resident did not want to pipe up with my Telluride learned technique that had worked 100% of the time.

Over an hour later, the doctors were perspiring, the patient was crying in pain, and with his shoulder still out of place, was sent to a hospital with his arm in a sling.

Yes, the fun and bonhomie reminded me of my Telluride Mountain Clinic stint –Telluride was just a different town, at higher altitude, farther away from a hospital, with slightly more relaxed alcohol laws and an actual town to walk around with many bars where you could find trouble. There is a sense that anyone (including doctors) working in a ski town, is essentially a ski bum finding various ways to pay for our days skiing on the hill. And that was somewhat true for me. I was also coaching the kids ski race team at snowbird on my days off so that I could receive a free ski pass. But otherwise there were not too many ski-town, ski-bum shenanigans to share with you—and if history was anything to go by, my ski town mischief, was anything but racy.

WHILE I HAD ENJOYED THE SKI-MOVIE ROMP *HOT DOG* (TALK ABOUT a film that cancel-culture could sink its teeth into!), I confess to an absolute dearth of similarly inspired escapades. In fact, the prior winter, I had actually been invited by a woman visiting town (we met previously at a mutual friend's wedding) to come out for a drink with her and her friends. Sure, I know how to go out and have fun in a ski town I thought. But really, after years living in a hospital, the few times I was let out to play seemed to illustrate my dwindling social skills.

I met her and her ten friends, all of whom seemed to be couples with nice southern accents, at a popular ski town bar. We later returned to their rented condo for another cocktail, which led to someone tossing out the idea of jumping into the hot tub. I know how to do that too.

Now, I didn't have a bathing suit because I had just come over to say hello and have a drink. "No problem," someone spouted, "Who needs suits?" Without enough thought, I took the statement literally, ran into the backyard and jumped into the tub in my birthday suit. A few minutes later five couples, and the very nice woman I barely knew, all arrived in their bathing suits.

Well this was an awkward conundrum. I could stay there all night. I could splash water in their faces and run out. And for reasons I cannot explain, I instead chose to stand up, showing off my small pasty white ass, and to walk to my car and drive home alone. I've never, knowingly, seen any of that startled group again, so, all's well that ends well.

You can easily see why I am writing a medical memoir and not steamy romance novels. Although maybe I should try fictionalizing a saucy Walter Mitty version of myself who does everything the opposite of what I did. Hmmm, *Playing Doctor Part XXX—My Thermometer Reads Hot.* I'll let that horrible idea percolate, and in the meantime, will share another super-fun task of residency doctoring life: Phone Call.

THAT SAME MONTH I WAS ALSO REQUIRED TO SPEND ONE WEEKEND acting as the mole. Recall my description of life as the mole from an earlier chapter? Well, I left out one element that plagued the existence of both the mole and the chief—it was called "Phone Call" and it sucked.

When you call your doctor at night or on the weekend, they have a "call" system. Your phone call is first picked up by an answering service, and then a physician is paged to call you back— maybe things have changed with cell phones. Pagers make us all sound like a bunch of drug dealers from the 1990s—which I suppose we were, depending on how you view the goods we were handing out.

So, when anybody decided to call their family practice doctor after hours, we sleep-deprived and still-in-training residents were present in the hospital to answer their late-night and weekend medical concerns—thus allowing the attending physicians to get more sleep. In theory, the system provided us with good practice in thinking through how to handle patients' worries over the phone. We learned to triage who could wait to be seen the following day and who should be told to go to the ER immediately. We learned to dole out acceptable medical advice over the phone at 3 a.m. as we simultaneously admitted sick patients to the ICU. Then we documented the phone call, our diagnosis, and our recommendations to the patient.

Before starting our third year we had actually participated in a ten-minute role-play training session where somebody pretended to be a patient calling to ask for pain medications to be refilled over the phone. This troubling request being the one we needed to be best ready to handle. Many, many people thought it would be easy to call over the phone and have a prescription for controlled substances, such as narcotics, sedatives or stimulants called to their pharmacy rather than the patient needing to go to the ER where the physicians knew them all too well.

The controlled substance phone call teaching can be summed up in several words: Tell them "No." That's it, teaching over. We were not allowed to call in controlled substances over the phone, so our options were limited to telling them no, no pain meds for you over the phone, and that they could come into the ER to be seen or wait and call their doctor in a few hours when their office opened. These statements were sure to go over well with people in pain or addicted to their medicine. I lost track of the number of times someone would call and say, "I just ran out of my pain pills and my doctor said I could just call to get some more." Or "I just ran out of Ritalin (an amphetamine type stimulant), and I have a test tomorrow, so I need them, and my doctor said I could just call for some more."

And we had the same answer every time, "Sorry, I'm not

allowed to call that in for you. You'll have to talk with your doctor in the morning."

"But she said you could just call some in for me."

"You'll have to talk to her about that not. I'm not legally allowed to call that in over the phone."

"So what good are you?"

A very good existential query, but regarding refilling controlled substances over the phone in the middle of the night, not very good at all. For all the other medical concerns, we used our medical training to make the right decisions.

I think patients thought they were being put in contact with someone whose only purpose was sitting by a phone waiting to give out free medical advice—sitting there, bored, just wishing patients would call with challenging medical concerns. But we were not sitting calmly on top of a desk in a Zen meditative pose waiting to take your call. On call nights, we were typically in the midst of high chaos and busy work (or perhaps dozing off for our five minutes of sleep that night), when the answering service paged us regarding a patient calling with hopes of speaking with their primary care doctor. It was in that frenzied or exhausted, woken from sleep state, that the pager would alert me to the phone service needing me to call.

I would call the answering service back and be greeted by the sweetest, happiest young female voice that sounded like she was about to break into a Broadway show tune, "Hello Dr. Lawrence, thank you so much for calling back. I have a call for you from Mrs. Jones about her nine-month-old daughter."

This answering service girl always sounded so ridiculously cute and friendly that I *almost* had a crush on her. I say almost, because in those busy and sleep deprived moments—and I knew she was only doing her job—I just hated her. She passed on Mrs. Jones' phone number and whatever pertinent information she had available about the patient's concerns. I groggily dialed the number and proceeded to listen to a stressed-out woman on the other end of the line, who was obviously disappointed that a mere resident was calling her back, wondering what to do about her nine-month-old infant who was crying.

"Nine-month-old kids cry. What's your problem?" was what I wanted to reply, but I feared the lawsuit popping up when I read the local headlines hours later regarding a nine-month-old infant dying of intestinal blockage after the parents were reassured by a sleep- deprived resident that it was normal for nine-month-old infants to cry.

Have you noticed how much the fear of screwing up maintained my level of dedication?

So I scoured my 4 a.m. brain and asked every pediatric question I could think of, "Is she feverish?

"No."

"Has she been sick?"

No.

"Has she vomited?"

"No."

On and on, wondering what medical symptom I was missing that could be dangerous.

Suddenly the mother volunteered, "She *was* treated for an ear infection today. Do you think the ear infection would make her cry?"

This is why I was woken up from my five-minute nap? I think I'm going to cry.

"Hello... Hello, are you still there?"

"Yes, but not for long. I'm sure she's fine. Good night." And I would go back to bed for another three minutes.

When people called on the weekend or at 4 a.m., you'd think it would be for an emergency or at least a pseudo-emergency. Here is a smattering of the phone calls I received when in charge of that emergency call system. What you are about to read are all true calls:

. . .

1) "MY HUSBAND HAS HAD TWO HEART ATTACKS RECENTLY AND HE had bypass surgery last week. He just began having chest pain and feels clammy and short of breath. He says it feels just like his last heart attack. Do you think we should go to the hospital?"

Based on the Darwin theories, my desired grumpy response at two in the morning sitting in the ER admitting sick patients was, *"Wait until the morning and go for a greasy diner breakfast. If your husband is still alive, it looks like someone wants him to live despite your close relationship with ignorance."*

Actual response: "I want you to hang up and dial 911, right now."

2) At 11 a.m. on a Saturday morning, Leroy, sixty-seven years old, called regarding his preoccupation with constipation. He had not had a bowel movement since yesterday and was very, I repeat, *very* concerned.

I went through all the usual questions to make sure it didn't sound like his intestines were blocked and told him he should drink lots of water, eat some fiber, and if he started having belly pain, to go to the ER.

Two hours later I was paged by the phone service and told that Leroy needed to speak with me immediately. I called him back and Leroy informed me that he still hadn't had a bowel movement. He had nothing wrong at all, i.e. no pain, no fever, no vomiting or diarrhea, but remained *very concerned.*

One hour later the phone service called and told me Leroy requested an immediate call back. So, I called him. Leroy then enlightened me with the news that he had gone ahead and given himself two enemas and, "...only a small amount of poop came out."

I had zero desire, at any hour of my life, to ever hear about Leroy's poop. He continued to report no signs whatsoever of pain, fever, or anything else medically concerning, and I told him that if he was really, really concerned, he should come to the ER and be examined.

At 11 p.m. Leroy called back to report no progress and that he was unable to sleep because of it.

"Go to the ER if you are concerned, please, please, *please*, just like we previously discussed," I repeated.

Fortunately, that night, Leroy never called back, and I figured he was either fine or had gone to the ER. Unfortunately, he would call me every day thereafter.

3) It was 3 a.m. and for the first time in more than seven days I was asleep at night when I was woken for this call: "I think my children might have lice, what should I do?"

Seriously? A 3 a.m. lice emergency?

"I...I don't know...maybe just call your pediatrician in the morning."

4) Early one Saturday morning I called a patient's number given to me by the infuriating, sugary-sweet phone service woman: "Hello, this is the doctor returning a call for--"

I was brusquely cut off by a husky female voice (decades-of-smoking husky, not sexy husky) demanding, "You need to tell my husband he needs to quit smoking."

"What? Who is this?" I replied.

The grating voice of optimal health hollered into the phone, "Wayne...Wayne! Get your butt on the phone, doc wants to talk to you."

What? No I don't. I don't want anything of the sort.

A voice I assumed belonged to Wayne-the-smoker then got on the phone, "Whadd'ya want?"

"I don't want anything. Your wife, or whoever the woman yelling happens to be, called me. I'm working."

I then heard him, politely muffling the receiver with his hand, bellowing to the concerned woman, "Bitch, yo! He says *you* called *him*."

Bitch, yo then got back on the line and yelled at me. "Tell him to stop! You're supposed to tell him to stop! The doctor said the smoking's bad for him, that's what you're supposed to do, tell him!"

I informed Wayne, "Smoking's not good for you. It's true."

Then they started barking at each other and eventually hung up on me.

5) The answering service paged me that Leroy needed an emergency call. This was the fourth night in a row he'd called with the exact same complaint of constipation, having had only small bowel movements during the day despite using multiple enemas. The first two nights I'd quickly called him back after hearing it was an emergency. The third night I had taken my time getting back to him.

Tonight I stared at the clock; it was almost 3 a.m. and I just did not want to call him. I was in the ER working to admit three sickly patients. The ICU had just paged me that one patient was complaining of chest pain, and another was becoming hypoxic (developing low oxygen levels). I had a ton of work to do and not enough time. Minutes passed, during which time the answering service called me two more times reporting that Leroy was calling them continually, wondering when I was calling him back.

I'd told him over and over and over again, "Leroy, you sound fine to me. If you're concerned, just go to the ER or go see your doctor tomorrow."

I finally called him back and listened to the gripping tale of his bowel movements for that day.

I then repeated the exact same advice, a bit of edge sneaking into my normally calm voice, "Leroy, I've told you every night, *every single night*, if you're concerned then just go to the ER."

Except now he replied, "Look, Dr. Lawrence, I may not be a doctor and I don't want to tell you your job, but it just doesn't seem right."

It's 3 a.m. and the only thing that didn't seem right was having a redundant conversation with Leroy about his bowel habits.

6) We received all sorts of pain medicine, or other controlled

substance calls; they had a variety of excuses ranging from, "My two-year-old just dumped my Lortab into the sink and I really need them," to "My dog ate my prescription," to "My mother-in-law just took my Lortab and I really need them."

The two-year-old in the sink excuse was vastly overused, and I felt I should be giving the callers lectures about the dangers of two-year-old children being given narcotic pills to play with in the first place. Same with the dog eating their pills, I would have been more concerned with telling them to get their dog to the emergency vet, except I knew they were lying.

Other excuses for lost pills: their purse was stolen (overused); their prescription was left in their pants pocket and went through the washing machine (overused), their car had been broken into and the prescriptions stolen (overused); and my favorite, the entitled: "My doctor always just fills them over the phone and said you would, too, so just call them in please."

I quickly tired of hearing all of these stories. And despite my emphatically consistent response that I was not legally able to call in prescriptions for pain medicine, they would call back throughout the night, hoping that I had either changed my mind, or that a more compassionate doctor would answer the phone.

I tip my hat to any creative soul inventing an original excuse for needing his or her narcotics refilled. I would seriously have loved to hear someone tell me purple-striped belligerent elves in wicked fast spacecrafts had vaporized their pills—I would almost have been tempted to call in a few pills for that level of bravado, *but*, as I told all those patients, repeatedly, I am not allowed to call narcotics in for you, no matter what.

And now, back to the call list:

7) I had a night off and when I saw the resident who covered my shift she informed me, "Leroy called last night, just like you said, right at 3 a.m."

8) "I'm nine months pregnant and my six other babies usually

delivered with less than an hour of labor. I've been in labor for like forty minutes. Do you think I should go to the Hospital?"

Why, oh why are you taking time to call me instead of rushing yourself to the hospital?

9) "My dog just shit on the floor, what do I do?"

I had no idea I was cross-covering for a carpet cleaning service.

10) "My daughter just got married and I really think someone needs to check her down there because her husband is huge, and I'm worried she might have been ripped apart."

So many things wrong with that call that I need not respond except to say it was not a prank call; I was there when the concerned mother brought her newlywed daughter to be examined by me in my clinic the next day. She (the newlywed) was fine.

———

I ALSO HAD SOME REQUIRED COURSE WORK IN BEHAVIORAL SCIENCE that month. Once more, the Behavioral Science course required me to sit and discuss how my own psychology affected my patient care. We cited difficult cases and discussed what we were feeling when, for example, a patient wanted more and more time with you during a visit when you were already running an hour behind schedule.

I felt the patients were selfish for being there in the first place when all I wanted to do was be outside playing. Yes indeed, there were a few issues to discuss regarding my attitude.

ALLERGIST ELECTIVE

HORRIBLE ROLE REVERSALS & MY WORST
PATIENT CARE EVER

The first weekend of February was marked by a riotous cross-country ski race I attended every year with a large group of friends in Sun Valley, Idaho. This was the one weekend I always requested to be free from call. And being allowed out of the hospital for this weekend consistently provided for joyous festivities as I temporarily returned to humanity with an abundance of zest and zeal.

Typically, I'd physically exhaust myself on the racecourse, then socially embarrass myself on the dance floor. The year prior however, had set an impressive low point for the bumbling duo known as Scott and John (that's me). We had just broken up with our respective girlfriends. Then the basement of our new house flooded as we tried to leave for the race, requiring a visit from a Hazmat crew. Scott then totaled his truck en route to Idaho. I proceeded to sprain my wrist slipping on ice during an impromptu bathroom break on the side of the road. Then, after the race, Scott lacerated his wrist while shattering an enormous gum-ball machine, and I made an ass of myself while wearing a wig and lipstick in front of my ex-girlfriend at the post-race dinner. The bar was not high for us to demonstrate any minute signs of maturation.

This year, perhaps as a sign of mild social evolvement, no major injuries or embarrassing situations occurred. The morning after the race, I planned to do my first long run to start training for my third marathon in as many years.

It seemed apropos that I ran a marathon every year of my residency and that they had mildly mirrored my years of training: the first completely unprepared. The second, despite being better prepared, went poorly due to it snowing the entire way. This final year I had decided to follow an 18-week training program, taking a serious, methodic, and healthy approach that would involve eating well, sleeping adequately, and decreasing my intake of cookies, caffeine, and French fries.

It was 13 degrees outside at 6 a.m. in Sun Valley on my first run as I nursed a whopping hangover. I did not feel healthy at all. But I kept putting one foot in front of the other, lungs burning with each icy breath of bitter air, as I tried to smile, imagining that this was somehow good for me. Hmm, I'll let you connect the dots, but seems a sniff analogous to my life as a resident.

When we returned from Idaho, the Winter Olympics were in town. Granted this has nothing to do with medical education and so I leave you with this message: if at all possible, attend the Olympics, they're inspiring and an incredible celebration.

During the games, I had elected to do a clinical rotation shadowing an allergy doctor. "Shadowing" has a sinister ring. Was I peering out from a cloud of dense fog, shrouded in a black cape, as though seeking potential victims for our pathology lab? No, all I did was stand innocuously behind the doctor, trying to stay out of his way and nodding approval when he explained what he was doing.

In early February there were not many allergens in the air, so the doctor's schedule was pretty light. This freedom from patients allowed teaching time on how to properly evaluate patients.

Allergists, it turned out, enjoyed very similar schedules to dermatologists, i.e. they had few, if any, emergencies and no call schedule. They looked in patient's noses and treated the offending problems with steroids, allergy pills, allergy shots, or the occasional antibiotic—even a resident had one-in-four chances of guessing the correct treatment plan.

Allergists had one special test that was critical to people with allergies: skin testing. Skin testing involved poking a patient with an array of allergens and waiting to see if their skin flared up to a specific allergy. I am certainly downplaying the role of the allergist —any patient or parent who sees an allergist is well aware of what an important role they play in keeping their life tolerable. I just do not have too much more to say about the topic as my focus was elsewhere that month.

My medical attention was challenged that month by my very own canine patient. Winston the 100-pound wonder pup had somehow ruptured the ACL in his left knee. I was barely cognizant of human anatomy and clueless that dogs even had an ACL to tear. They do and they are expensive to fix. The surgery itself sounded barbaric. Somebody calling himself an orthopedic vet would saw Winston's tibia bone in half, spin the bone around, and screw it down backwards so that there was less pressure on the ruptured ACL.

Then the challenging part for the two of us (the dog and me), a brutal recovery. Eight weeks confined in a pen (the dog and frequently me) and slowly extending walking distances over eight more weeks.

Suddenly the roles were horribly reversed. I was no longer the doctor telling patients everything would be fine or telling a parent how to take care of their sick or injured child at home. Instead I was the nervous and overwhelmed person being sent home from a doctor's doorstep with an invalid patient and being told everything would be fine.

But it wasn't the least bit fine. I had questions: How did he walk? How did I get him to the bathroom? How did I know if he was in pain? How was I to move a 100-pound dog up and down the stairs for several months? The situation was not ideal for either of us.

After I was initially informed that he needed the surgery and realized that I would need to care for him throughout the recovery, I had stood silently in disbelief—I still had to show up at work in the hospital. Then they told me the price of the surgery and I went into shock. I did not want Winston going through surgery and being in pain afterwards. But beyond compassion was the simple reality that I could not afford the surgery. I did not have two grand for this surgery, and for some inane reason he was not covered under my insurance. But he needed the surgery, or he would continue limping in pain. Were these feelings similar to what parents went through on a regular basis? I began to feel I was a terrible dog owner, not able to afford what my dependent dog needed.

Tail tucked between legs with shame, I called the credit card companies and begged for a credit increase. Unremarkably, they thought that was a great idea.

Hats off to all you parents (and dog owners) who face taking care of those young kids and pups. It is so easy to be the doctor and take care of the acute illness or surgery and to assume that everything else will be fine at home. I began to recognize, however little I wanted to, that the care *really* started when the patient left the clinic. Adapting injuries and illness to real life, paying for it, taking care of someone sick, someone in pain, making it all fit around work schedules, school schedules—that's where the hard work comes in.

The day of surgery arrived, and I dropped Winston off at the vet. I guess he knew something was wrong, as I was shaking, and he started shaking too. Do you parents go through this every single time you take your unsuspecting child into any experience that will hurt? (I learned the answer to that question myself after taking our kids to their doctor when they were younger).

Kind of an interesting fact, if you've ever taken an animal to the vet, it's common for them to shake and act nervously. Apparently, they are able to sense all the other stress hormones from the previous animals that have been treated or put to sleep. Makes me wonder how much humans also pick up those stressors in clinics and hospitals? Back to me now:

Later that day I picked Winston up, and the true trial started. Here is my first email to friends:

"Thank you all for the letters of support, dog cookies, and overall concern. The good news is that Winston seems to be recovering quickly. The bad news is that he is recovering quickly. He is a terrible patient and very demanding, refusing to eat unless I sit in his pen and feed him by hand--except for cookies and treats which he is willing to eat without coercion. Subsequently I have spent a great deal of time in a dog pen the last week. His communication skills are also completely lacking. At his age I would expect a smattering of effort on his part to help me differentiate his whines for attention from those of needing to go to the bathroom, being in pain, declaring this situation sucks, or my water is too warm. So I must always opt for the bathroom run—which is, in itself, a slight ordeal because I must support his hind legs with a towel looped around his belly. You would think this surgery would slow him down – instead he charges forward with me still trying to loop the towel under his waist, slipping in the snow, at which point my shoe comes off and he does three spins to wrap the towel and leash between both our legs and his belly-- then he tries to urinate. That was the successful journey.

The other ventures result in his rolling in the snow and trying to run, usually at 3 a.m., while I give adamant commands: 'You're the patient. Listen to me! I know what's best. I do. Did you hear me?' At some point I actually believe I can convince him of these truths.

Yesterday he was slightly too excitable, jumping on my bed, jumping on me. I cannot believe this is good for his leg (although, in complete frustration, I tell him, 'Fine, if you think that's good for you, go ahead and do it,' before I remember that I am supposed to be responsible for this two-year-old, and cannot afford a second surgery.) So, after chew toys, bones, and a very long discussion did nothing, I turned to western vet medicine and gave him a sedative. I returned one hour later to find him looking very doped up. This seemed like a good plan until I tried to walk the weaving, punch-drunk, three-legged patient. I am no longer a big fan of the sedatives. Anyway, the honeymoon is over--in fact it ended by the time we returned from the vet the first day when I strained my entire back carrying him down the stairs and proceeded to step into his water-bowl, smacking it into my shin and spilling the water everywhere. He howled, I wanted to cry, and instead spent the night in a funk not sure how I was going to make it all work, amazed at all you parents that make it work every day. I have next week off and in case you need me, I'll be in a dog pen working on a film script. I am sure Shakespeare worked though writing blocks in a dog pen. Thank you all, only several months left!!

Kisses and licks from the pup and from me as well, yours infirmus cannus."

Eventually we developed a daily and nightly routine that neither of us really enjoyed. I was experiencing medicine from the other side of the exam table and not enjoying it one lick.

Given Winston could do little more than lie around and the Olympic games were in town, I decided to take time away from playing Florence Labrador-gale and went to see the sporting events with a scheduled week of vacation.

I was having a great time taking a break from my clinic and canine-nursing duties until one afternoon, walking up a hill to see the men's Giant Slalom ski race at Park City, I noticed that I was having a difficult time breathing and had to stop halfway up a short walk due to the pain in my chest. Recall, I was training for a marathon, so walking up a hill was not typically a gasping-for-air-inducing challenge. The lovely woman I had started spending time with was close friends with ski legend Bob Beattie, and we were going to sit with him for the race. But I didn't think my excitement at meeting this icon of the sport was the reason for my breathlessness either.

Later that night I became feverish and started coughing, which caused sharp burning pains in my lungs. I figured I had pneumonia, influenza, or both.

For days I lay on the couch taking some antibiotics and worried that the week off from running was going to destroy my marathon-training schedule. That was how I spent my vacation week. Eight days later I tried running on a treadmill and just about collapsed, running at half the speed I used to warm up at. So, this was what being sick felt like. I was not enjoying the gifted opportunity to learn patient empathy firsthand, not one bit.

DESPITE THE ONCE IN A LIFETIME THRILL OF THE OLYMPICS BEING IN town, caring for a recovering dog, training for a marathon, and taking care of my own sick self, I was still required to see my clinic patients—and with my secret executive probation status, I had zero wiggle room. This month I had the dubious honor of starting the chapter in what would become my most humiliating case of inappropriate medical care.

Once upon a time, a cute woman appeared in my clinic. It turns out that I knew her, sort of. I'd been friends with her mother and sister years before—which turned into one of my excuses for why her case turned out so poorly.

She came to see me complaining of back pain and requesting pain medication. Should that complaint be a clue? No, we should treat every patient individually, with an open mind, and without prejudice.

Come on John! Really?

How many times have I written about the enormity of the red flag that goes up with patients complaining about back pain? Many times. Many, many, *many times* in both books one and two I wrote about patients with chief complaints of "back pain" being a red flag to doctors. But alas, I was a sympathetic doctor, ready and willing to help my friends—or sisters of distant friends long since disappeared, in this case.

This lovely appearing patient had been examined by an excellent sports doctor prior to seeing me. She had however, been out of his care for several months—which was why she thought she was having the pain again.

I immediately suggested we get her back to seeing the same doctor that had so brilliantly relieved her pain the first time around.

She replied that she had become disconcerted with that doctor's opinions of what she would have to go through to get better and had left his care.

Wake up John, that's another warning flag, you bozo.

I rationally re-proposed that she return to that prior doctor because, as she herself had pointed out, she had actually improved under his supervision. But she was currently in tremendous pain and told me they were unable to schedule her to see that doctor any time soon.

Alarm bell. Ringing loudly. Are you listening?

No. I am not.

She batted her eyelashes and told me that I was probably the caring and compassionate type of doctor that could make her better.

Which of course, I was.

I agreed to step in and offer my own medical evaluation and treatment for her sore back.

When I examined her, she had some very tight muscles in her upper back, all of which caused her tremendous (subjective) pain when I touched them, but otherwise no findings that were concerning. I was very aware of how easy it was for patients to tense their back muscles and say they were sore—but she seemed to genuinely be in pain with really tight muscles.

Since she was sort of a friend by acquaintance, I figured she was being up-front with me, and I agreed to prescribe her some pain medication until we received the results of an MRI scan. In the meantime she was to start physical therapy.

All of the above treatment plan was good—just not the pain medication part. Bad move, bad, bad, bad. Bad.

One week later she called to request a refill on her pain medications.

"Is the medicine helping?" I asked, stepping into her perfectly laid trap.

"They help *sooo* much, thank you. I only take them when I need to, but I feel so much better. You are such a great doctor!"

Seriously John, are you completely oblivious to the red flags madly slapping you across your face?

Yep.

I felt warm and fuzzy and unsuspectingly wrote her another prescription for more pain pills. Then I asked how physical therapy was going.

"My babysitter cancelled, so I couldn't make it, but I rescheduled for next week," she replied. She was a single parent, and I was a caring, benevolent doctor, sympathetic to single parenting needs.

Over the following weeks the babysitter canceling morphed into her car breaking down, forgetting the appointment, the physical therapist canceling, and something to do with her back hurting too much to be able to go to physical therapy.

Simultaneously to excusing herself from physical therapy, she began requesting larger prescriptions of pain medication so she could avoid paying repeated co-pays. This request seemed reasonable to me, as she was a single, working parent with financial concerns.

Then she requested a longer acting pain medication, specifically, Oxycontin, so that she did not have to take the pain medication as frequently. She batted her eyelashes. And remarkably, that request also seemed to make complete sense.

Given how many paragraphs I have previously written about recognizing drug-seeking behavior, I expect you have rapidly identified several warning signs that should have been going off like air-raid sirens in my head. But I was dealing with an injured dog and sick lungs. And did I mention she batted her eyes at me?

Months later I was called into my advisor's office to be interrogated about a young woman he'd seen while I was away for a few weeks on a clinical rotation. He'd been dubiously impressed with the volume of pain medications she'd requested and had promptly declined her request for another prescription.

Last I knew she was in jail.

I eventually, and quite embarrassedly, apologized to her mother, feeling like I had been an accomplice to her daughter's narcotic-abusing and dealing behavior. The mother was unaware of my role in the case and knew that I'd been trying to help her daughter's supposed pain.

Regardless, I found my role as the duped candy man to be somewhat repulsive—used and tossed aside without so much as a written apology from the story's femme fatale. Not even a call or card from prison. Good riddance.

P.S. Note to any future patients: Don't even think about batting your eyelashes at me, I'm totally onto you now.

NEWBORN NURSERY

CIRCUMCISION, MACHETES &
MANSCAPING (WAYS I DON'T WANT TO DIE)

The following month was spent in the newborn nursery caring for babies along with covering the labor and delivery deck every third night in order to keep the nursery well stocked, i.e. more newborns to care for. How cute, right? No. In the nursery your squished and wrinkled pooping machines are reduced to numerical nightmares:

How many ounces are they eating?

How many grams of weight have they lost?

How much weight have they gained?

How high was their fever?

What was their bilirubin count?

Why did the nurse keep calling me to come see if I thought some kid was shaky?

Why did he have a temperature?

What dose of antibiotics should we order?

Nightmarish numbers aside, the nursery was actually a very easy place to work if the babies were healthy. But it quickly became an overwhelmingly busy place if a single newborn was sick or had any abnormal risk factors, like being an underweight newborn, or a premature infant, or twins, or anything outside the ordinary. Having two or three not totally healthy kids in the nursery meant spending every hour watching their vitals, their labs, their breathing, their weight, and washing my hands in between seeing each kid. This month provided if nothing else, terrible chafing of the hands.

Beyond keeping accounting tabs on the tots, we senior residents were also responsible for performing the occasional circumcision.

Circumcisions had become a point of medical controversy as there seemed to be no evidenced-based studies proving there was a medical benefit to circumcising defenseless newborns. Welcome news for all you two-day-old boys picketing to stop the cutting. I had, however, in clinic, evaluated several six to ten-year-old patients who began having infections underneath their foreskins. They were miserable little boys because it hurt to urinate, and their penises were swollen. They became *really* miserable little boys after a painful circumcision that they were old enough to remember forever. Try telling one of those unfortunate lads that there was a controversy about early circumcision.

Performing circumcision early was actually quite simple: we strapped the kid down (which rightfully made him cry), stuck a sugarcoated pacifier in his mouth (to stop the crying) and injected local anesthetic around the head of their penis (re-ignite loud crying).

After the injection-induced wailing, however, most infants promptly fell asleep. There were several different methods to proceed with the rest of the job. One was a guillotine-type tool that just lopped off the foreskin. Urban legend-type rumors circulated of residents accidentally lopping off the head of the penis along with the foreskin when using this Robespierre-inspired device. Fearing for the children as well as my own finger should the gadget misfire, I opted to never once lay hands on such a contraption.

The next method was a little safer, as it involved placing the penis in a metal protective helmet clamp. I recommend not allowing parents to watch the procedure.

The one time, however, when a parent with a guilt-induced desire to witness their namesake's mutilation stayed to watch the procedure, is the only time the event ever had issues. I erroneously, on all counts, reassured the concerned father that kids normally slept through the operation, and that his child's skin would be totally numb so he would not feel a single thing. Father and son looked at me with doubtful stares, and to make a point of making me look like a big fat fibber, the kid screamed the entire time we were together, from start to finish.

I strapped him down, he cried. Gave him the pacifier, he spat it out, and cried louder as the dad stared at me, convinced I was a throwback barber surgeon. I injected the numbing lidocaine and the kid somehow shrieked even louder—we're talking non-stop piercing hysterical shrieking. The father was close to dialing a child abuse hotline.

I placed the helmet clamp on the patient's apparently not anesthetized penis and the kid burst eardrums in all the surrounding townships. I looked around to make sure the father was not about to clock me with a blunt object. I then turned back to the task at hand: secured the clamp over the head of the penis, and cut off the foreskin, all the while listening to horrid cries from this small unit of screeching lungs. But the circumcision was done.

Or so I thought until I loosened the clamp—the very clamp that was supposed to compress, and thereby stop, any bleeding.

The clamp was not being very effective at its job, as the penis was unquestionably, for new father and apparently incompetent junior-doctor (that's me) alike to witness, actively bleeding. The bleeding would not stop. The kid was crying, his penis was bleeding profusely, and the father now appeared to be in the corner schizophrenically lambasting himself for allowing this ancient ritual of brutality to occur and glaring at me with serious malice. Meanwhile, I was worried that I'd cut too deeply into the foreskin and had disfigured this child, sending him out to a life of locker room taunts...that is, if he survived and did not exsanguinate in the room.

The attending physician covering the nursery finally looked into the room to see why I was not back out taking care of my other duties.

Without giving away my very real concerns, I told him, "No problems, just a little excessive bleeding." I glanced at the father, realizing too late that the words "excessive bleeding" might legitimately cause concern, and I quickly attempted to cover myself, reassuring the father, "But it's not that much, really, just a little bit more...*excessive* than, uh, usual."

The attending started to walk out, "Oh, I'm sure it's fine. Why don't you just finish up –"

"Actually, since you're here, do you mind taking a look?" I quickly requested.

As the attending ambled closer to examine my bleeding outpatient, I whispered, "Does it look alright to you, I mean, *does everything look normal?*"

Completely ignoring my hints at subtlety, the attending blurted out for all the nursery to hear, "Don't worry, I think it looks fine." And then he walked out.

I tried smiling at the father.

Despite that far-from-glowing reassurance from an actual doctor, one who hadn't performed a circumcision in decades, the father still seemed skeptical. I didn't want to attempt any reconstructive surgery and opted to wrap the penis in gauze, wrap the kid in a blanket, and hand him off to the visibly pissed off father.

Welcome to the world, kid.

(Of note: weeks later I followed up with the family practice resident who took over the infant boy's care, and he let me know that everything looked absolutely healthy and normal. PHEW!!)

WELL, THAT WAS NOT THE BEST SELF-ENDORSEMENT. BUT SINCE THE door is open, let's step through for some more embarrassing moments.

I freely admit upon writing and mentally reviewing that particular circumcision that it was not, despite good intentions, my finest moment. Gratefully the infant did not bleed to death in the nursery, and as mentioned, managed to heal quite well—a testament to his good genetics and not my skill. Had anything worse happened in the nursery that day, I'm quite certain I would have dropped dead with a sympathetic heart attack. Not how I wanted to die.

Kicking the proverbial bucket due to sympathy for a circumcision gone wrong seemed a bit anti-climactic. Over the years there were far more exciting incidents when I might have died: avalanches, bike vs. car/rock/road accidents, surprise storms while rock climbing, eating hospital cuisine—all far more adventurous ways to move on. And there were also certain episodes where I thought quite clearly: *This is not how I want to die.*

Recall, if you happened to read *Playing Doctor Part One*, that Scott (the cycling mad individual who biked hundreds of miles with a deflated lung for laughs, and who was arrested multiple times before turning into a boutique lawyer) and I had travelled to Italy during our time skiing in the French Alps. It was in Italy that I became sick, avoided seeing an Italian doctor as he hacked up disgusting phlegm, and returned to France to meet Dr. Lacoste who helped steer me towards a medical career path.

I left out the vast majority of our mountain antics: some beautiful moments in the high peaks of the Chamonix Valley, some exciting escapades, and plenty of humiliating ones, because this is a medical book. However, our jaunt to Italy one chilly February, after hitchhiking from Chamonix and arriving in the hills outside Florence, was notable for our reception at the villa where we planned to stay with a university friend overseeing undergraduate students studying abroad. He seemed excited to see us, offered us some water, and then informed us that we could not stay in the villa. Anyone hosting un-invited guests would be sent home—a punishment which had already befallen several students.

Ce ne c'est pas une probleme! We lived in the high mountains of France and were accustomed to braving cold weather. Given we were somewhat broke, we took an offered blanket (a thin, crochet type, with more holes in it than material) and attempted to sleep on the stone slabs of a nearby alleyway with that one piece of flimsy material to share. But there was no sleep. We just lay, frozen on those icy slabs of chilled rock. There are few times in my life I have ever been so cold. I kept imagining that I must be on the face of some Himalayan mountain. And while we lay close to hypothermic, huddling together under our decorative sofa throw, it occurred to me that we were cuddled together in the town of Fiesole.

Fiesole is a very romantic and historical destination that you can visit from Florence, just take bus No. 7 from the central train station and you'll arrive at the piazza surrounded by cafes and restaurants. The town was a quintessentially charming Italian place which at the time also boasted of being home to a serial killer. *Welcome to Fiesole, we have a lovely church, Etruscan ruins, and our very own serial killer. We hope you enjoy your stay.*

Amorous couples frequented Fiesole to enjoy the hillside vista with a picnic of paninis and wine. But for years, a local farmer would occasionally sneak up on these lovebirds and hack them to pieces with a machete. I did not want to be hacked up anywhere at any time with anything.

Lying awake I realized we were likely going to freeze to death or be chopped up and everyone back home would think Scott and I were lovers. Regardless of which option brought about my demise, neither denoted a way I wanted to die. Somehow, we survived the close to hypothermic night, avoided the murderous farmer (it was probably too cold for him to be out stalking love-birds), and our fortunes turned skyward the following morning—fodder for a future book perhaps. And if you're planning a trip to Fiesole soon, the farmer was eventually arrested, so you can now sleep easy on those cold and worn stones.

More currently however, I almost succumbed to a more real danger, and it was yet another way I did not want to die. This "event" occurred during the editing of this book and was far more medically relevant (although, I suppose macheted limbs and hypothermia do have a place amongst medical literature) and dare I say, slightly more embarrassing.

What happened?

Manscaping. Manscaping happened.

I did not even know manscaping was a term, but I googled it and it is.

I do not want to die manscaping.

I was partaking in the act of manscaping with an electric razor that said it was designed to not cut you. And in one distracted moment I managed to prove them quite wrong. Just cleaning things up down under, not really paying attention, when suddenly a sharp bite like pain immediately re-focused my attention as the floor of the shower turned bright red.

Holy shit.

I did not have much more intelligent thoughts beyond that two-word expletive as I realized my wife was arriving home any minute with the kids from school. I certainly did not want my impressionable young children seeing blood all over the shower, nor all over our towels, or the floor (by now there was blood everywhere) or seeing their dad soaking wet bleeding from his mid-section as though he had been castrated. I looked for something to stem the bleeding and clean up the mess. All the towels were white.

Why, oh why, are all our towels white?

I can't use those towels. My wife will kill me before I bleed to death.

I found a thick roll of gauze and held it tightly against my exsanguinating scrotum. Within seconds the entire roll of gauze turned dark red, saturated with blood, and started dripping all over the bathroom tiles—another major faux-pas I needed to quickly clean up before my wife arrived and killed me for ruining the flooring.

Holy Shit. Again.

I went through another roll of gauze…then another…and another…the blood was flowing so rapidly that I could not even see what the cut looked like beyond the fact that it was somewhere on my scrotum. (How many readers did I just lose? Most?).

I couldn't quite figure out what to do, so I packed on more gauze, put on a pair of the tightest compression shorts I could find and cleaned up the bathroom shower and floors that looked like the Fiesole serial killer had found me after all (not a real concern, as mentioned he had been arrested years back).

I walked quite gingerly around the house after the kids were home, nervous about moving the rolls of gauze. And there was *no way* I could ask my wife to look at the bleeding site. As anybody with kids knows, they can't hear twenty-three shouted commands to get dressed for school or to go to bed, but somehow have a preternatural ability to overhear the one faintest whisper regarding anything of small consequence that you quietly try to share with your spouse. There was no way I wanted them mis-hearing me and then telling the entire school that their dad sliced off his own balls.

Finally, desperate to arrest the bleeding, I sat on the toilet and tried to locate the damaged site as blood flowed at rates capable of being measured in barrels per day. I was all too aware that people tend to exaggerate how much they are bleeding, but this was becoming significant. In all my years of repairing injuries, I had not seen this much blood loss apart from serious traumas or during surgeries in the operating room.

Squeezing skin to stem blood flow I eventually located the

laceration: a two-centimeter vertical slice through a blood vessel. I needed some serious pressure to stop the flow. With almost 25 years of medical experience under my belt, what did I do? I clamped gauze over the injury using really strong metal clips that we had in the house to close potato chip bags. They hurt, but the bleeding finally stopped.

I waited an hour, by which time I was in a good deal of pain from the clips and figured the blood had clotted. I gently removed the clips, waiting to see what would happen and...*WHOOSH*. Blood streamed down my leg, creating rosy puddles all over the floor.

HOLY SHIT!

I repeated the chip clip process three more times, waiting as long as I could, only to have the bleeding continue. Alligator chip clamps back in place, I lay in bed fretting… could I leave the clips on overnight? *No.* They hurt and I started to worry that they were cutting off blood supply to the skin of my scrotum. I did not think (a relative term when you are worried about bleeding to death), that a necrotic scrotum would work favorably towards a marital sex life. (How many more readers did I just lose? My kids certainly just slammed the book in the garbage).

I took the clips off one final time, hoping, hoping, hoping the blood had clotted...*NOPE.* Puddles of blood re-filled the pants down around my ankles.

Finally my family went to sleep. I lay in bed wondering what to do. I had to do something. I couldn't live with the chip clips on, they really hurt, they would potentially turn me into a eunuch, not to mention they looked awkward pressing out from my pants.

I was going to bleed out. But there was just no way I wanted to die like Pentangeli in *The Godfather* or Gianna in *John Wick 2* (before Wick's intervention), bleeding out from sliced blood vessels in a bathtub.

This was not how I wanted to die.

I needed to go to the ER.

Nope. Not going.

I was not going to die in my sleep bleeding out from a manscaped scrotum and have that issue forever traumatize my kids when they found me the next day in a bed that looked like the famous horse head scene from *The Godfather*.

But there was also no way was I going to the ER, waiting in line at midnight to explain what happened to some disinterested and likely cute receptionist. No. I would not do that. I could do this myself. I had to.

I gingerly climbed out of bed, took out an old set of suture equipment, found some really old suture thread with a giant needle—*hold up, not that one, that needle is huge...where's the small 6.0 small thread used for delicate work...found one, phew.*

I got out a lot of gauze, sat down on an absorbent pad we used to potty train foster puppies we care for, and took off the clips.

Blood flowed freely.

I set to my task trying to see better with light from my iPhone. This was a total disaster. Where to start. What if I stick this needle through my scrotum and punctured another blood vessel? I'd have to call 911. I was now sitting in large pools and clots of blood.

Am I getting lightheaded?

Do I need a blood transfusion?

I have to do something. Fast.

I stuck the needle through the skin. Then I encountered a new obstacle. Over the last year my eyesight, perfect for all my life, was not quite so sharp up close anymore. *Damn.*

I got up with a suture thread poking through me, trying not to pull it back out, blood dripping as I worthlessly pressed gauze against the wound, and waddled to find my reading glasses.

I finally sat back down donning my readers...still not great for seeing thin blue suture material against a background of blood flow. The situation was becoming hopeless. I started to think about heading to the ER.

One more try, find that damn suture!

And I did, I found the thread, tied some knots and the blood flow seemed to slow a fraction.

I took a deep breath of relief. More sutures, more difficulty seeing it...but finally I could see the damaged vessel better and using *Slumdog Millionaire* like knowledge from *Playing Doctor, Part Two* (learning to tie off the bleeding artery in an 82-year-old woman, who had fallen at a basketball game, with a figure-eight suture), I used a figure-eight suture on myself. I then placed four more sutures to fully clamp down the blood vessel, and finally the bleeding stopped.

Taking out those tightly-tied, tiny suture threads a week later, hoping not to re-start the bleeding would be its own uncomfortable issue, but for now I had saved a mortifying trip to the ER, avoided traumatizing my kids, and did not have to wear those blasted clips anymore.

I eventually went to sleep, albeit uneasily. If the bleeding re-started overnight while I slept, I would be found lying dead in a puddle of my blood. Should I write down what happened so nobody came up with a weird account of me dying from some fetish gone wrong? The truth was already stupid enough. I passed out and hoped for the best. But no, not how I wanted to die.

Was there a lesson in all this?

Don't shave distracted?

Include chip-clips in first-aid kits?

Buy stronger reading glasses?

Tell your wife when you're bleeding to death?

No, no real lessons at all.

And yes, I did finally tell my wife (once the kids were back in school the next day). She already thinks I'm a bit of a bozo so why not confirm her beliefs.

And P.S. what did she do? Well, apart from laughing at me for being an idiot, she told a friend of hers who just happened to make TikTok videos for the rival shaving company. So, they interviewed me, and the resulting videos have over 3 million views. This is my life.

CARDIOLOGY

I'LL NEVER BE A CARDIOLOGIST—BUT I KNOW WHEN TO CALL ONE

Cardiologists are super smart doctors. They completed four years of medical school, then ranked so highly during three years of internal medicine residency training to be accepted to an extremely competitive fellowship study in cardiology which typically lasts three *more* years. So, after a decade of intense training, it's mildly understandable that a few of their brethren like to let residents know just how smart they are.

I was a family practice resident and there was no way I was ever going to be as intelligent in the care of the heart as a ten-year trained cardiologist. On top of which, I was still scarred by my very first medical school clinical rotation, which happened to be cardiology. At that time I did a piss-poor job of learning cardiology as my efforts had been entirely focused on survival (mine, more than the patients). So I had some very real hesitations about finally scheduling a required month of cardiology training.

Despite my own reservations on the topic, cardiology remains a critical specialty because it deals with your heart. We consider the heart to be an essential organ for functioning in daily life (modern politics occasionally leaving the point debatable), and yet we abuse our heart in so many ways. Let's face it, as the world's most overweight population, U.S. citizens treat their hearts like 17th-century bastard stepchildren.

The physical heart plays a somewhat crucial role in pumping blood and oxygen around the body—both currently indispensable to being alive and conscious. Yet we choose to make our hearts work so hard, filling our blood vessels with fat, not exercising, and eating poorly. With the sheer number of people suffering strokes and heart attacks, heart disease has maintained its place atop the podium as the number one cause of adult deaths in the USA for decades. So, cardiologists are not only smart, they're also really busy as there's no lack of heart disease to treat.

Granted, some people were handed the genetic short-straw in the heart health category, but for the vast majority, the idea of preventative medicine runs counter to traditional Western medical care. Preventative care seems to contradict a national desire to be comfortable and not fix what isn't broken. Oh man, I'm on the soapbox now:

The problem with things like high blood pressure, high cholesterol levels, eating processed fast-food crap and processed sugar, and not exercising, is that you might not going to feel anything wrong until one day when you fall over and feel an elephant standing on your chest, or you start slurring your words and cannot feel part of your face. Congratulations, if you survived, you just altered the quality of your life, and likely that of your friends and family who will now need to take care of you *if* you happened to survive the heart attack or stroke.

Given the prevalence of heart disease, the residency program agreed the heart was not only important to staying alive, but also a frequent and important reason that patients sought medical care. In response to that dazzling insight, they issued a mandate that all residents must complete one full month on a cardiology service. This was essentially a month-long sentence to join a cardiology team and work long hours back in the hospital with in-house call nights, i.e. working overnight in the hospital and on weekends.

Most other family practice residents had decided to get this required elective out of the way during their intern year, piling on all the most challenging required months at once and thereby clearing the last year for fun electives without call. I would like to write that I held off completing my cardiology sentence as I knew cardiology was crucial to my post-residency knowledge and therefore wanted it fresh in my head when I graduated, but I think you know me better by now. I put it off until my third year because I never thought I would actually finish residency training.

Now, with my final year of residency winding down, I still hadn't fulfilled this dreaded requirement—dreaded now because I correctly predicted any cardiologist would treat me like an intern and prove my worthlessness as a resident, as a practitioner of medicine, and as a human being. The imposter syndrome was firmly planted in my mindset.

As an intern however, I might've been granted the benefit of the doubt for not knowing too much, but as a senior resident about to be treating my own patients, they would expect me to know what I was doing. Worst of all, as mentioned, cardiologists are super-intelligent and work really hard. They round at the hospital early every morning and would expect me to do so as well. It simply would not do for my third-year schedule, or for my marathon training, to wake up early and go to the hospital to be chastised for my unwavering ignorance regarding the love of their life, treating problems of the heart.

I scoured my brain for alternatives and came up with an idea to approach the cardiology department at one of the larger hospitals where a cardiologist had organized a team to study the heart in connection with fitness evaluations. Despite continually injuring myself attempting to stay healthy, I liked fitness and figured with this team's friendlier work schedule, we were meant to be together. Regardless of my matchmaking vision, it was highly unlikely they would allow me onboard—but for some reason they agreed to let me join the team and I danced a merry jig. I did. Literally. I had just dodged working a miserable call schedule in exchange for some nine-to-five type work.

Our role was to perform cardiac evaluations on people undergoing fitness testing. These people spent the morning at different stations where they underwent a variety of tests including blood labs, cholesterol levels, a nutritional consult, body fat analysis, and a treadmill type stress test. My group was in charge of the latter.

We calculated the person's VO2 max with a very complex math formula, then measured their waistband with a measuring tape. The cardiology team was doing a clinical study to evaluate if a person's waistband size could be proven to predict heart disease risk. Our results? It looked to be overwhelmingly directly related. So, everyone with a big waist, you have a higher chance of checking out early with a heart attack or dealing with the aftermath of a stroke than those people with skinny waists. And the rest of you don't get off so easy, you get to pay for their medical care.

My elective choice turned out to be excellent. I did not have to arrive too early in the hospital, as we only tested in the late mornings, and there was no overnight or weekend call schedule. We asked patients a few questions about their health, shaved their chests (male patients only), applied ECG leads, watched the heart monitor while they ran on the treadmill, took their blood pressure and heart rates at different intervals, and then discussed the outcome of the whole exam.

People were embarrassingly out of shape. Granted, I was accustomed to a circle of friends who thought running and biking several hours a day was fun and normal (this was before they had kids).

Every morning several corporate individuals showed up in workout clothes and headbands to be put on the treadmill. The treadmill was programmed to increase the speed and angle of elevation every three minutes. During that time we watched the electrical activity on the EKG and monitored the person's heart rate and blood pressure. I found it amazing how few people could get past a slight jog or even a walk. The local population appeared to be in truly terrible shape.

While the person on the treadmill struggled to breathe, our work was pretty simple--unless something went wrong, such as the EKG monitor telling us that the person was not getting enough oxygen to their heart (i.e. they were having a heart attack) when they were required to do more than walk. Otherwise, we stood and cheered the people's efforts, trying to get them past a jog, pushing them to challenge their physical limits without falling off the treadmill.

Meanwhile the cardiologist would discuss heart issues, EKG tracings, and acute and chronic care of cardiac patients with me. I really enjoyed these friendly, un-pressured fireside type chats.

But then the cardiologist must have been contacted by my cantankerous residency program because he suddenly changed our stress-free learning environment into quizzing me on EKG readings. He subsequently realized that my knowledge was not only far below his, but closer to that of a poorly educated child. So he assigned me books to read, EKGs to study, and scheduled a final exam together. Then he was called out of town.

I took my chances and bet on black in an imagined game of roulette—which, in this case, was that he might forget about the exam. I did study several of the most common EKG tracings but didn't crack the books and crossed my fingers he wouldn't return in time to quiz me. The ball rolled and landed on . . . black! I escaped without facing an inquisition of the heart and had more time to train for the marathon—which was more aligned with preventative cardiology in the first place, right?

Are you starting to see a pattern? If I got through med school, then, yes, you too could go to med school, work hard, and do well.

And while I make light of my time on the cardiology service, I am not dismissing that it's critical for primary care doctors to understand. By this time, I could easily identify the most common and concerning EKG tracings. On top of which, I would immediately send anyone with a hint of heart problem directly to a hospital or cardiologist. I was never going to insert a catheter into someone's heart, so the emphasis on spending time with cardiologists in a catheter lab didn't make much sense.

If I was ever unsure about an EKG reading, I would consult a cardiologist. If a patient needed heart treatment, I would send them to a cardiologist. In fact, if there was anything ever uncertain about a patient's heart, I would send them to a cardiologist. But the residency program figured the best way for us to learn about the heart was to spend time with the heart specialists being quizzed about complex heart issues we would never treat. Go figure.

YES, INTRICATE HEART PROBLEMS REMAIN A MYSTERY TO ME, BUT I am familiar with the importance of protecting the heart. Consider, for a moment, that on a strictly physical level, we know what's good for our heart health and what is bad for it. For example, there's no question that eating saturated fatty foods takes a toll on the workings of the heart (and plays a negative role in a multitude of other problems, ranging from diabetes to depression). And yet the fast-food industries thrive, and the U.S.A. continues to grow fatter. The U.S. government subsidizes the sugar industry, knowing full well that processed sugar increases the rates of diabetes, heart disease, depression, obesity, and the plethora of health conditions that accompany them. And then there's sugar's many benefits to the health care provider's bottom line. Unhealthy people boost the health care economy, as more and more of the GNP is put into caring for people's poor lifestyle choices, thus providing doctors with job security. It's just not supposed to work that way.

So what's the problem? As a population, we've been told that eating healthy is good for the heart – the physical heart. But what about the spiritual heart? Turns out, caring for the spiritual heart benefits overall heart health as well. The California-based cardiologist, Dr. Dean Ornish, is famous for his studies demonstrating that our physical hearts do much better when we have healthy and supportive relationships—and enjoy purposeful living. He has published many books supporting the fact that in addition to a healthy diet and aerobic exercise, being loved, having support from family and friends, can actually *reverse* heart disease.

Benjamin Franklin noted that we all take our health for granted until it is taken away. Think about that over a cheeseburger.

While all the above was a bit of gratuitous lecturing on heart health and lifestyle choices, I now want to loudly applaud cardiologists and their medical teams for their treatment of my own heart scare:

Early one morning I woke up feeling discomfort in my upper back and neck—which is normal for me with a history of injuries. It was still dark out and a bit cold, but I figured if I went for a run, the blood flow would loosen things up.

I started running and my chest immediately felt compressed in a vice with pain radiating into my neck and ears. I could barely breathe due to the pain. But I've been relatively healthy all my life and was convinced I could run through it. I headed out to some trails in the hills, miserable and in pain repeatedly telling myself, *I am not having a heart attack. This is not a heart attack.*

I was not sure I would make it home but was convinced that if I could run for over an hour, then it could not be a heart attack. I doubt that self-imposed heart attack test is found in typical medical textbooks. I made it home and decided not to go to the ER, just feeling miserable, unable to breathe well, and in pain. The next day I still felt very uncomfortable and weak and finally decided to call one of my doctor friends. Far wiser than me, he immediately demanded I head in for an EKG at his clinic. Maybe he paid more attention on his cardiology rotations.

Minutes after the EKG was taken, he was rushing me to the hospital as a cardiologist thought I needed to be taken to the catheter lab for a likely heart attack. That was the first time it hit me that just possibly something serious could be going on, but I still mentally refused to accept it. I had three kids and a wife, and I planned to spend a lot more time with them over many more years.

To end the story, the final evaluation came back that they thought I likely had pericarditis, inflammation around my heart from a possible virus (this was right after the pandemic started so I underwent many covid tests—all negative). I had to keep my heart-rate low for three months, and to take medicine during that time to keep the inflammation down—I like exercising and I don't like taking medicine. But I did as I was told as I was informed that if I didn't, the inflammation could recur and cause permanent scar tissue to form around my heart. I went from being able to run or bike for hours, to feeling short of breath walking very slowly to the mailbox.

A year later, all turned out completely fine. My heart scans and tests were all 100% healthy. I remain very grateful to all the amazing and knowledgeable heart doctors, and their teams, caring for me and making sure there was nothing cardiac-related that could take away any future time with my wife and kids. And they were all super-nice, fun people who did not make me feel like an idiot. Like I said, I really was scarred and traumatized by my third-year medical school experience. Regardless, another massive thank you to all the hard-working cardiology teams out there who keep us ticking!

THE EMERGENCY ROOM

THE FRENCH ART OF USING INSULTS TO
REMOVE YOUR APPENDIX

As a resident, if you absolutely needed to miss work, there were protocols in place that allowed another family practice resident to cover for you. I unsuccessfully attempted to follow those protocols when I traveled to a wedding during my intern year but was nonetheless permanently placed on top-secret, executive probation for missing my pediatric shift. So if you asked me, the system had flaws.

A resident from my family practice program had covered the shift I'd missed for the wedding, and the pediatric hospital appeared to work just fine without me for one day. My reputation did not fare as well, and I was still placed on the silly *Animal House-*inspired probation despite the pediatric chief resident informing the residency programs that I had both requested and been approved to miss that day. Well, nobody said resident life was fair.

Aside from my personal mishaps—about which I apparently still harbor some bitterness all these years later—shift-coverage usually went smoothly. If needed, you asked a fellow resident to cover for you in the hospital, and in return, they asked you to cover a similar shift when they wanted a day off in the future. So I was occasionally called in to staff the nursery, mole duty, or ER for another resident. We helped each other through these hectic years that didn't offer days off to go to weddings, to the dentist, to have your snow tires changed, or some other fun event, such as staying home if your dog or kids were sick.

You were typically only asked to cover an overnight shift when you were on a less demanding rotation without call nights so as to avoid being overburdened. I always showed up way more relaxed and friendly when I was only covering one single night, rather than facing the millstone of a full-month of call and weekend shifts. A single night awake on the wards was stress-free to handle at this point. And being more relaxed meant you could focus on some of the nuances otherwise missed when stressed. The following are notes from one such ER shift:

The truth about the Emergency Room is that the majority of cases are a far cry from what I believe most people would classify as minor disturbances, let alone true emergencies. Slivers are not emergencies. Bunion pain is not an emergency. A urinary tract infection (in an otherwise healthy adult), while it might feel like one, is not usually an emergency—at least not on par with a child not breathing, someone bleeding to death, the ozone layer depleting, or last call at a bar on a Friday night.

And for all you doctor types baying at that statement—yes, I know, urinary tract infections, especially in the elderly population, can result in true emergencies leading to mental status changes and even sepsis...fine, so put UTI's in the elderly on the list of possible emergencies—but I think you understand what I'm saying. The ER is often, especially pre-Covid era, used for simple doctor visits by people who do not want, or cannot get, an appointment at a regular doctor's office.

The ER had inefficiently (at least for costs) become the primary care giver for many patients, and the only place to go after typical office hours for medical care. Urgent Care clinics have popped up around the country, which has taken some of the strain off the ER, but they continue to be overwhelmed and underfunded by virtue of treating so many common colds for people who then refuse to pay their medical bills. The Covid Pandemic certainly altered people's desire to show up in the ER for such minor cases, but I guarantee there are still patients showing up in the ER because it is the closest place to home.

Is your child having a runny nose for twenty minutes a true emergency? No. But I've repeatedly evaluated that runny nose complaint for concerned parents.

Is chest pain an emergency? It can be. The ER remains the place to treat or triage patients with potentially serious conditions. Ideally patients are evaluated, treated and, if advisable, sent home to follow up with their primary care doctor. But first, a patient presenting with chest pain has to be properly assessed to rule out more immediate and potentially dangerous diagnoses, such as a heart attack.

How do you work through these problems? You go back to fundamental medical school training, i.e. History and Physicals. The majority of diagnostic considerations are made by asking relevant questions and documenting appropriate (hopefully) answers. Then, if a heart attack remains a concern, labs are ordered, such as blood tests, x-rays, EKGs, and with all the acquired information, ER doctors decide which patients they can treat, which can go home and which to admit to the hospital. And what constitutes an emergency really does remain in the mind of the sick or injured.

Is breaking your hip or femur an emergency? Yes.

And so are the potential complications of hip fractures. If your femur breaks and a piece of bone pierces your femoral artery, you will likely bleed to death without rapid intervention—so death is one potential complication.

Patients admitted to the hospital with femur fractures are often immobilized and therefore at risk for blood clots (deadly), pneumonia (deadly), and boredom (deadly). Furthermore, patients with fractures are often started on narcotic pain medications, which can cause severe constipation (ouch), which leads to hemorrhoids (more ouch). We admitted numerous patients to the hospital for constipation and for hemorrhoids. Another exhilarating side effect of pain medication is urinary retention. You will be more aware of your bladder than ever before if it is unable to empty.

Constipation, hemorrhoids, and urinary retention are all potential stressors in any relationship—stressors which could lead to divorce (more stress), attorney bills (more stress), and taking a mid-life crisis trip to Jamaica where you get stoned and arrested (which sounds stressful too).

That above list of complications (and this is just a theory) might explain why a sixty-seven-year-old patient with a broken hip decided she did not want to risk being taken to the ER the night I was covering. When the ambulance transporting her to our hospital ER stopped at a traffic light, she leapt from the vehicle and somehow managed to run off down the street for several meters before being stopped.

An equally plausible theory for her attempted escape is that she found out I was working in the ER that night —take your pick.

Ok, enough with the hip fracture diatribe. People showed up every day with these minor ailments and I suppose they keep the Emergency Rooms solvent. Apparently "emergency" is in the mind of the insurance cardholder.

What constitutes a true emergency? If you said, "not breathing," I'd say you are right. Not breathing is a true emergency. When Scott's lung collapsed for the second time, his future-wife, Rachel, dragged him into the ER because she was tired of him complaining and not breathing well when he attempted to exercise. At the University Emergency Room, Rachel and Scott waited in line behind an ER frequent flier patient named Vicky who wanted narcotics because her bunion pain was flaring up.

While my friend sucked air into his one remaining lung, Vicky bawled that her bunions were sore. Vicky was then treated emergently, while my friend sat in the waiting room at risk for a potentially fatal tension pneumothorax, being told by the triage nurse, "You probably have a bellyache and need to learn to be patient while the doctors treat real emergencies."

Despite Scott's somewhat poor treatment in the emergency room (to be fair to the triage nurse, Scott had completely normal vital signs, i.e. normal heart rate and normal blood oxygen levels), what really pissed me off was that he had just completed a 109-mile mountain bike ride faster than I could ride with two lungs. I suggested to the ER docs that we just leave his lung deflated in order to level the playing field.

Vicky's plight, a depleted inventory of narcotic pain medications, remains a common reason for ER visits. I suppose the frequent visits for narcotics means that those meds must generate a lot of revenue for emergency rooms, which is helpful, as many of them operate in the red. However, death from prescription drug overdosing has actually exceeded death from recreational drug use over the last years, which is significant enough to warrant a few more notes on pain-pill-seeking patients.

Ironically, large hospitals have pain clinics established where they dictate how quickly physicians should hand out recurring prescriptions for controlled substances. It's a cash cow as the patients must return regularly to receive frequent refills on their meds; then their insurances are regularly billed for the addictive medicine being handed out like Halloween candy. But when those patients came into the ER, they were treated with a bit more skepticism.

Everyday, people came to the ER seeking pain medication—many of them in pain, many addicted to pain medications. And the groups were not exclusive to each other. Doctors in the ER therefore had to figure out who really needed those types of drugs and who was abusing the system. Despite it being a felony to lie to physicians about narcotic drug prescriptions, and despite being warned, the same people showed up every week, sometimes the same day, with new, sometimes self-inflicted, often imagined, injuries and pains.

They repeatedly demanded narcotics to relieve the unbearable agony of their twisted ankle, the severity of which prevented them from sleeping. The lack of sleep from the pain caused them to be late for work and at risk for losing the job they needed to feed their children.

Their entire existence and family's subsistence all hinged upon our humanity and willingness to write a prescription for narcotics —and if I could be so kind, a note excusing them from the last week of work due to their twisted ankle, even though they stated the injury only occurred two days ago (all real conversations).

Frequently, their supposedly debilitating ankle displayed neither swelling, nor bruising, nor a shred of evidence to support the ankle had ever been injured. These patients literally thought we were short order cooks, standing around waiting to write pill prescriptions and work-excuse notes.

The typical conversation, when I explained the discrepancy in timing, ethics, and logic of their request, went something like this:

"Doc, look, I *originally* injured it *two* weeks ago, so yeah, it already got better."

"Bill, it seems you have a mildly sprained ankle. Why don't you take some ibuprofen, ice it like we discussed, and we'll get you scheduled for physical therapy."

"Can I get something for the pain?"

"That's what the ibuprofen is for, and you can take some Tylenol as well, if it gets worse."

"But I can't sleep at night. Aren't you going to help me get some sleep? I can't work because I can't sleep."

I loved the implied guilt, that it was my fault they couldn't work.

"Bill, this is a twisted ankle that you've already managed to walk on for two weeks. It's not the type of injury that warrants narcotics."

"It got worse. I just need something to help me sleep for a few nights."

"Have you received any pain medication in the last six months for anything else?"

"No. I hate taking pills. I never take pills. I haven't taken a single pill in like, five years, not even an aspirin."

"I'll be right back." And I would walk out and order a DOPL (Division of Occupational and Professional Licensing) report. The DOPL report was a list of controlled medications the person had received over the previous months. I could then go back into the room and ask Bill again.

"So you haven't had *any* prescriptions for pain medications in the last six months."

"Nope."

"You sure?"

"Yup. I hate pills. I don't even take Tylenol."

"Well it says on this report I have here, that you've had seventeen prescriptions for Lortab (the narcotic pain medicine enjoyed by Rush Limbaugh) in the last two months and twelve for Percocet. Some of these you got from different doctors on the exact same day. Do you know that it's a felony to lie to me about controlled substances?"

"Those aren't mine."

"Well, the prescriptions have your birthday, your name, and your address on them, so I'm pretty sure that they are."

"I lost my wallet, someone's stealing my identity!"

"Then we should call the police, don't you think?"

"No...I think it was my cousin who borrowed my wallet."

This was a highly routine conversation in emergency rooms and unless it was a really big abuse, the police did not have time to follow up on small time narcotic abusers.

Years later, working in Urgent Care clinics, I had those identical, waste of all our time conversations, every single week.

AN EXAMPLE OF A SOMEWHAT LESS ROUTINE CONVERSATION WAS with Sherrie, a woman who came in with an elaborate story of a sore back that had just flared up. She only needed some pain medicine to make it through the next few days until she saw her back doctor. She repeatedly denied having taken any prescription pain medications in the last six months.

I examined her back and then we discussed the plan to treat her pain: "Sherrie, it looks like you have a strained back." Then I explained all the proper care of using ice, heat, ibuprofen, and scheduling her for a physical therapy appointment.

"And I would really love something for pain," she piped in.

"Yes, of course, and that is where we have a problem. You told me that you hadn't received any pain medications in the last six months, right?"

She stared right at me, "Yeah?"

"Well you have, haven't you?"

"What?"

"Had pain medication prescribed to you?"

"Huh?"

"Sherrie, you went to a different clinic just last night and received a prescription for pain medication. You've received over 300 narcotic pills in the last month, alone, often from different doctors and occasionally from different doctors on the same day."

"So?"

"So, that part when I asked you several times if you had received or taken any pain medications in the last six months, and you repeatedly said you hadn't, you were lying to me."

A really long pause from Sherrie as she shoots daggers at me with her eyes, followed by, "I didn't hear what you said," in a tone implying I was an asshole for accusing her of lying.

"But if you didn't hear what I said, why did you answer my questions?" I replied.

No response from Sherrie. Instead, a frighteningly glacial stare at me that actually makes me nervous that she was about to attack me.

Finally, I broke the silence, trying to be helpful, "Do you think you have a problem with narcotics, Sherrie?"

"NO!"

Then she hung her head and just stared at the floor for a minute. I didn't know what to do, still fearful she might attack me like a cornered hyena. Instead, she began bawling deep guttural sobs. I waited for her to stop, which she finally did. And then, she just sat in a catatonic state, still as a statue, staring blankly ahead as if the whole situation would magically disappear.

I slowly backed out of the room, still convinced she was about to pounce and rip off my accusatory head. I returned minutes later with a pamphlet on getting help for addiction.

For every person you'd ask if they wanted help with addiction, over ninety percent stormed out cursing your existence; most of the rest said it was impossible to get in anywhere for help, and very rarely, someone took you up on finding help. Sadly, of those that did, most were back next week asking for more pain pills, saying the rehab didn't work, that they couldn't get seen, etc. The system was not, is not, well equipped to handle addiction. It's very difficult to help people who, as addicts will admit, can only help themselves. You cannot do it for them. Fortunately, there are more addiction centers opening up, gradually, and more promising treatments will become available soon.

BESIDES NAVIGATING THE CRAFTY PATIENTS WITH DRUG-SEEKING behavior, we did see a few other medical problems in the ER. Given the mostly high stress level that people brought with them to the ER, communication was a key ingredient in being a good ER physician. Eager young physicians were trained not to use "doctor" talk with patients, as it was confusing and misinterpreted in calm circumstances, let alone during a stressful medical emergency.

I barely understood medical terminology myself, at times, constantly looking up commonly bandied words, and therefore had little expectation that my patients should understand it, either. There were studies demonstrating that the majority of what doctors told patients was missed, misunderstood, misinterpreted, lost amidst a barrage of information, lost in a high-tension moment, and lost in translation.

Foreign language translation was a definite communication obstacle. I could order dinner in Spanish (often receiving something different than what I thought I ordered), could convey simple requests, like asking a bartender to bring me another beer, please, and could ask where to find the bathroom in a very nice Spanish accent.

Despite my very mediocre Spanish (at best), and even more flimsy dalliance with French, I was frequently deigned the Spanish speaking *expert*, depending who else was on the shift. I was often called into a patient's room and described as the Spanish-speaking doctor—and I freely admitted I had no idea what was being said 70% of the time. I don't know what they did when there were Spanish-speaking doctors who lacked my whopping 30% comprehension rate.

On top of my not really understanding the language as well as I would like, my decent accent fooled many patients into believing I could actually understand them, which made them speak to me at two times normal speed instead of the half speed I normally required to pick up individual words.

As almost everyone knows, your deluded ability to speak any language dramatically improves when you drink alcohol. But showing up with a six-pack of beer at the start of each shift to speak better Spanish likely wouldn't have gone over well in our largely Mormon state...or possibly anywhere.

So I would try to only ask simple questions, like, "Does Octavio have a cough?"

And the parents of Octavio Herreras, a feverish infant, would ramble off a long answer assuming I could talk their talk. I would listen and try to pick out the occasional word from: "fiebre... tos... diarres... vómito," but I was making a fifty-fifty, piss-pot guess if they had said that the child actually had that symptom, or not— either of which made a significant difference in what we would choose to do next.

At least with Spanish, I had a smattering of words to fall back on. The other languages encountered in the ER, such as Russian, Vietnamese, or Sudanese Arabic, I couldn't even fake well and instead resorted to a family game of charades.

Despite coming from far away and exotic places, the patients were still expected to bring some basic communication skills to the table. But I think, on occasion, there were patients and doctors in the room who were nodding their heads at each other as if they understood what was being said but had no real idea.

Now, all was not lost, we were legally required to have a translation service available (this is pre-smart phone, pre-Google translate, etc.). And we would occasionally try and use the system if there were no English-speaking family members present to help translate. But reality made it hard to wait for a translator to call you back when a patient was miserable, bleeding, vomiting, or barely responsive.

I would ask people something simple, and hope that perhaps a family member could interpret most of the words, such as "Have you had any surgeries previously?"

Which is actually an important question to ask because if a patient had already had a surgery, such as having their gallbladder removed, it was pointless for me to pursue the possibility that their abdominal pain might be due to an infected gallbladder, since they did not have one.

Additionally, a history of surgery on their abdomen increased the risk of adhesions (scar tissue), which increased the possibility that their presenting stomach pain was due to a dangerous obstruction, i.e. their intestines were blocked off by the scar tissue throughout their belly.

So it was a good question: "Have you had any surgeries in the past?" And there were really only two answers: Yes or No.

An affirmative answer brought up more communication challenges:

"Do you remember what type of surgery?"

"Well, let's see, when I was a kid, I think my mom said they had to fix something, because I remember I was knocked out."

Is that helpful? No.

"Anything else?"

"Nope. Just that one when I was a kid."

"Ok, no other surgeries."

"Oh, wait, there was this other time, I was having pain, and you wouldn't believe it, these doctors couldn't figure anything out, I saw like three different ones, and finally this really cute gal orders a scan, and the next day, they take out my appendix."

So, "Yes" answers required work, because you had to write it all down, not the part about the cute gal or the three different doctors, just the surgery. And that semi-difficult-to-interpret response was in English, so just crank up the level of challenge when any other language was involved.

"No" answers were typically much easier to handle.

If they replied, "No," to the question of prior surgeries, I still wanted to be certain, and would ask a second time, "So, just to be sure, no surgeries?"

And patients typically looked at me like I had a hearing problem before replying, "No, none."

But I always remember this one French patient who spoke English perfectly well after having lived in the United States most of her adult life. I knew she spoke English perfectly well because after I tried using my smattering of French to introduce myself, she scornfully told me how much better her English was than my French, as she'd lived in the United States for a long time—and I bet she had lived quite condescendingly as well.

But I was suspicious of some deceit and asked a third time, "So, no surgeries, ever?"

To which she looked at me like I was crazy and repeated, "No. None." She then spoke French to her husband, using a sharp tone that clearly indicated she was telling him how stupid I was, or that my head was shaped like a turnip—my French was not as good as my Spanish.

Minutes later I examined her belly for the tremendous pain she was experiencing in her right lower abdomen. I explained to her that it was possible her appendix was the source of the pain, although not likely, but I was going to order some blood tests and an X-ray to start.

"That diagnosis is not possible," she informed me (in a very haughty tone).

"Why not?" I asked, perturbed that she believed her medical skills, like her French, were better than mine.

She sneered down her Gallic nose, snootily explaining, "Because I had my appendix taken out years ago." *You silly excuse for a ridiculous twit of a doctor*—is what I was convinced she was saying under her missing beret.

I wanted to shake her and ask, in my non-existent French, *Did your snail-eating compatriots perfect the art of performing appendectomies using verbal abuse and sharp doses of arrogance instead of surgery? How the bloody hell was your appendix taken out without the use of surgery? And don't blame it on translation issues because you've already tried humiliating me with how much better your English smells than my French!*

But instead I just smiled—and pushed a little bit harder in her right lower abdomen to make sure there was no appendix there (which you can't really feel anyway).

(P.S. -- I really like France and my friends there, but she was just a riot of fun to deal with that day. Apparently, I have some pent-up issues regarding her attitude.) So, yes, beyond a lack of language skills, there were also the really tough communication barriers, like ignorance, stupidity, and no fucking clue—for which I can blame myself in many circumstances, but some patients gave me a run for the prescription.

How could I be expected to properly treat patients when our conversations, almost consistently, went something like this:

"Do you take any medications on a regular basis?"

"No."

"OK. So, no medical issues or problems for which you take medicine?"

"No."

"Do you have any illnesses or chronic medical issues?"

"No."

Then, I'd read further down their medical chart, and discover, *hold on just a minute—*

"Wait, I'm sorry, I noticed it says right here, in your chart, that you take Norvasc?"

"Yeah."

"What for?"

"My high blood pressure."

"And it also says you take an aspirin a day?"

"Yeah."

"When did you start taking aspirin?"

"After my heart attack."

"So that bit about not taking medicines or having any illnesses was a ruse?"

"What?"

"Exactly. And the bit about not having any chronic medical issues?"

"I don't."

"What about the high blood pressure and heart attack?"

"Yeah, I told you, I take medicines for those, so I'm good."

No, you're not, you silly Muppet.

As if we needed to be medical detectives to make the job of unraveling what was wrong with patients any more challenging. The ER was starting to make me believe that common sense was an endangered commodity.

What the ER provided was an opportunity to see all sorts of crazy stuff, learn a variety of medical skills, and to witness, first-hand, that despite our opposable thumbs, we are not a super-intelligent species. Yes, certain teams have created rockets to the moon, mere generations after making fire. But the majority of us are not rocket scientists, and too many still enjoy playing with fire. Literally.

One day I walked into the trauma room to evaluate a patient whose chief complaint was a burn on his face. The patient lay in the exam bed wearing a one-piece workman's suit and Elmer Fudd-style hunting cap. His buddy stood next to him wearing a matching suit and cap.

"So, how did you burn your face?" I inquired.

Turns out that he and his partner in fashion and wisdom had been hanging out at home on this fine Saturday and thought they smelled gas leaking. The gas line, however, was under the sink, and was difficult to visualize in the dark. You need a source of light to see in the dark.

Hmm, what is a good source of light?

Fire?

Correct! And what's a good source of fire?

A cigarette lighter?

Yes!

After that logical mental exercise, it's understandable why our patient opted to use a cigarette lighter to better illuminate the possible source of gaseous odor.

The Elmer Fudd-Looney Toons hat suddenly seemed quite apropos, as this guy currently resembled Wile E. Coyote after a rocket exploded in his face, complete with blown-back, charred hair and burnt eyebrows. Fortunately, nothing too serious seemed to have occurred physically, so I continued with the interview, one part of which was to ask of any previous illnesses or injuries we should be aware of.

His reply? "Well, I shot myself in the foot with a nail-gun last week."

I could not help laughing when I called the Burn Unit to discuss the case, as it did involve the patient's head and neck, and I needed them to evaluate the injuries to make sure there was no likely swelling that could cut off his breathing later in the night. (Burns around your face and neck can trigger a myriad of possible complications, including cutting off your breathing due to an inflammatory response.) But it still seemed funny. The burn unit was accustomed to evaluating these types of accidents—and from my time as a medical student in the burn unit, I can attest that there was no lack of people looking for gas leaks with cigarette lighters.

Then I recalled all the times in my life where I'd survived some similar, albeit stupider, incidents, and stopped laughing—granted, I had been closer to ten years old at the time.

ELECTIVE STUDY MONTH

WHERE I SEEK MY REVENGE AGAINST HIGH ALTITUDE MEDICINE

n unknown, but in my opinion, brilliant individual created the idea of an elective reading month for our residency program. The original intent behind this "reading" month was to create a workable opportunity for maternity leave, or for parents to spend time with their family while studying for their medical board exams. The elective stuck around as residents started using the option to delve deeper into medical topics of personal interest that they hadn't been able to study to their heart's content during the otherwise busy years of residency.

What type of medical issues would residents want to study with this elective month of study? I imagined giddy residents choosing to study something racy, like pre-obstetrics in the tropics, complete with treating the resultant STDs or malaria. Or perhaps straining elbows while investigating the effects of golfing on blood pressure? Or maybe probing into the bends while scuba diving in the Caribbean? Or... well, I can't really think of too much more that people would want to study, but it's out there.

Regardless of the original intent, when I discovered this magical month of reading actually existed outside my imagination,

I chortled with joy and re-danced my merry cardiology jig. This elective was a vacation in the guise of studying. This option could keep me away from hospital duties for an entire month. Would they let me study some outdoorsy and fun medical topic without being beholden to their structured clutches? I'd damn well find out.

I CHOSE, AND WAS APPROVED TO STUDY, HIGH-ALTITUDE MEDICINE. First of all, it sounded cool. Secondly, if I was to study high-altitude, I should probably go to the mountains. I love the mountains. Thirdly, it provided an opportunity to hang out with my doctor friend in Telluride who had already made movies regarding his own high-altitude medical studies on Mt. Everest.

Lastly, I needed to vindicate a horrendous lecture I once gave on high-altitude medicine—in fact, it's a gross misrepresentation to call it a horrendous lecture. It was more of a rambling slew of words related, at times, to altitude, lungs, and the brain. I had presented that disastrous lecture to the Medical Intensive Care Unit (MICU) team at the V.A. hospital during my second year of residency. I opted not to share that tawdry showing in the previous book as you readers already had enough ammunition to bring to a medical board regarding my lack of physician-like skills.

It's probably only fair to now recount those several minutes of time in the V.A. MICU; time which several doctors and nurses will never recover in their life and for that loss, I apologize profusely.

Unlike the University MICU, where all the patients were extremely sick and then immediately transferred to a regular hospital bed as soon as they demonstrated any hope of improvement, the V.A. MICU had a slightly different patient population. MICU patients at the V.A. were acutely aware of the benefits of having a private ICU room with nurses and residents at their beck and call if anything went wrong. So it was almost impossible to convince patients they were ready to be transferred out of the ICU and to go share a room, and more importantly, a TV remote, with another patient.

We residents started having debates if the patients were heating their thermometers to fake fevers in order to bluff their way into staying in the privileged ICU setting rather than being kicked to the V.A. hospital floor (which, to be fair, scared me too).

The V.A. MICU was commanded by a relaxed and genial attending who enjoyed hiking and skiing on the same mountains where I played on my time off. The rotation was going smoothly, as we had common ground to discuss besides feeding tubes and extubation trials (where we took the intubation tube out of a patient to see how well they could breathe without it). That was until the same attending decided that all residents were required to present a morning lecture.

Regrettably, I decided that High Altitude Pulmonary Edema (HAPE) and High-Altitude Cerebral Edema (HACE) sounded like fun and interesting topics to present. "Regrettably," as I would soon discover that the same attending had published multiple papers on the subject without telling me.

I did have a personal interest in these medical risks of traveling at high altitude, as I enjoyed climbing and skiing. If you're high up in the mountains and don't give yourself time to acclimatize properly (allow your body to get used to being at higher altitudes with decreased levels of oxygen), then you can feel sick. First you start feeling nauseated, weak, and headachy. Congratulations, you have developed Acute Mountain Sickness (AMS). AMS was something I had frequently treated working in the Telluride mountain clinic as the town is situated 10,000 feet above sea level.

The treatment, if a person is seriously sick, is to immediately transport them to lower elevations. which makes them feel better. If it's not possible because you are in a rocky wilderness at night during a blizzard, or perhaps dealing with stubborn vacation people who don't want to leave the fun of a wedding rehearsal dinner, then you can try hydrating the patient and giving them a diuretic medicine that helps restore the acid-base balance that was created because they were breathing rapidly to try and get more oxygen into their system.

AMS is commonly seen at elevated altitudes where people fly to vacation in the mountains and like to party (i.e. dehydrate themselves) without acclimatizing. HAPE and HACE, however, are not common and are far more serious. These are conditions whereby your lungs and brain fill with fluid (edema). The suspicion is that HAPE occurs when blood vessels in the lung constrict due to low oxygen levels and thereby squeeze fluid out into the lungs. When your lungs fill with fluid, well, no surprise, you don't breathe well, and you can die.

HACE, even more complicated, occurs when low oxygen levels trigger a cascade of reactions in the brain, which leads to fluid leaking from the blood vessels into the cerebral tissues. It, too, leads to bad situations such as confusion, somnolence, and death.

So rapid diagnosis—such as quickly recognizing pneumonia versus HAPE, which have similar presenting signs and symptoms but different treatments, is critical. See, this isn't so difficult to understand. That's also not the in-depth level of discussion I would be expected to bring to a morning lecture as a medical resident.

In the MICU, in between ordering courses of antibiotics for the patients and futilely adjusting their ventilator settings, I had printed off several novels worth of articles regarding HAPE and HACE—I even glanced at the pictures in a few of them. However, as the weeks passed by, I was filled with genuine glee that it appeared our attending had forgotten I hadn't given my presentation and in partnership with his memory lapses, I forgot to read the articles.

On one of my final ICU mornings, however, as I strode happily through rounds, knowing my ICU time was almost done, he shockingly recalled that I had yet to enlighten everyone with my lecture.

"Since we wrapped up early, let's go hear John's morning report. I'm looking forward to this one."

What? No! I'm not ready. How do I get out of this situation?

I tried improvising, "I'm sure everyone's busy, I can wait and um, do it later? Or a different day? Mornings are always so busy for morning report with uh, morning work still to do?"

Shit. I was already rambling.

"Nonsense. This is a great time. The conference room looks empty, let's go."

I'm doomed.

Internal alarm bells were ringing to run away as I gathered my stack of unread articles feeling anything but the enthusiasm the attending was displaying. I considered running for doors shouting there was a coding patient in the cafeteria—compared to what lay ahead, it would have been far less embarrassing to sprint to the cafeteria and look confused as to why there was no choking patient awaiting a Heimlich maneuver .

Our small team moved into a hot and cramped conference room, where I was somewhat relieved as there would only be five people hanging their heads at my unplanned discussion. Then some MICU nurses who were scheduled for the conference room after we finished popped their heads inside.

And the attending invited them to stay for, "...what promises to be an interesting exercise in learning about the effect of altitude".

They too sat down, unaware of what a horrific and mumbled waste of time was about to beset their day.

I looked at my notes, started speaking and nothing coherent fell from my lips.

I held up pictures of lungs and brains and made random statements about mountains and pressure. I commented on the "badness" of lungs filling with fluid, the "badness" of brains filling with fluid and at the same time could feel the badness of fluid accumulating in my crotch as sweat poured down my body.

Had a medical student given this lecture, it would have been considered unacceptable. Had a junior high school student presented this mess, he would have been commended for making a decent effort. But I was neither, and as the perspiration increased to sub-tropical levels under my scrubs, I hoped that maybe I would suffer a small heart attack to save me from further misery and embarrassment. Glancing up at a clock, I realized my long-winded fumbling mess had only taken up eighteen minutes and I needed to talk about something for another twelve. I began to pray for a code to be called. *Please, one of you bastard patients I've helped keep alive, have a cardiac arrest before I do.*

No such luck, we had treated our patients too well, and at the current moment, they were surviving better than me, enjoying their breakfast of pancakes in bed.

Minutes later, agonized by the cacophony of muck I was spewing and tired of interrupting me to correct my nonsense, the attending called the lecture over and recommended I actually read his articles. His disappointment was clear over my remaining time in the MICU where instead of sharing our usual banter, he chose to completely ignore me.

So now, a year later, I had good reasons to learn from an expert in the field. I looked forward to my weeks at altitude in Telluride.

My plan to learn about high altitude medicine from my Telluride friend, Dr. Hodo (one of the world's experts on the subject), however, suffered a bad turn when he decided at the last minute that he was *not* going to be in Colorado during the month of April.

Never one to be put out by simple logistical concerns, I found the good twist on the bad turn. Since Howard was going to be in California instead, editing a movie he was submitting to the Mountain Film Festival, I could join him there. Tricky turn on the good twist—he was not exactly sure when he was going to start editing, as he first had to visit his sick mother—damn. Stupid illnesses continued to plague my happy existence.

So I worked on a screenplay, trained for the marathon, and

suddenly the month was over. I reviewed my previously disastrous presentation on high altitude pulmonary/cerebral edema from the MICU all those months before, read some textbooks and considered myself more of an expert on high altitude medicine than the other family practice residents.

Coming full circle, many years later, my friend, Paralympian and all-around amazing human being, Chris Waddell, invited me to be the doctor on an expedition as he attempted to be the first paraplegic person to summit Mt. Kilimanjaro unassisted, using a hand cycle. Of course I accepted. Then I realized I needed to review high-altitude medicine as Mt. Kilimanjaro is 19,341 feet above sea level. When I looked up facts about altitude sickness on that mountain, and learned that every year people die there from altitude sickness, I realized I was vastly underprepared.

I called Howard again to receive his expert advice on how to prepare for the trip. Instead, we missed each other's phone calls. But I reviewed many notes and books until I felt competent and packed all the appropriate high altitude and wilderness medicines.

And on the night we planned to summit the mountain, camping at around 15,000 feet above sea level, many neighboring tour groups had people exhibiting signs of altitude sickness. Rather than resting before we started our summit climb, I walked between tents handing out treatments and evaluating people in different camps to make sure their lungs were clear, their brains functioning, and that everyone was healthy enough to attempt the climb.

And hours later, on top of the mountain, the sun rose from below us and it was absolutely magical. See, it all worked out in the end.

THE ADVENTURES OF DON
UNDER MY SCALPEL

WHERE I REMOVE A VERY SHAKESPEAREAN
AMOUNT OF FLESH

By now you've realized that I do not rate myself anywhere on the list of the worlds amazing, let alone average, doctors. However, one of the few areas I will say I do a good job is suturing. I was fortunate to have learned from great teachers over the years, starting with an orthopedic surgeon friend who invited me to spend the summer between the first and second year of medical school assisting on cases at the Shriner's hospital. Every operation required the patient's skin be closed, i.e. sutured shut. And I was given the instruction and task to suture, over and over, under the watchful eye and blunt commentary of the OR team.

Years down the road (and I'll share one story later), I felt quite confident in my abilities to do fine suturing work on patient's faces to repair messy lacerations. However, before reaching that modicum of self-belief, I still had some learning to undergo. Herein is the story of putting Don back together again.

Don was a great guy, in his late sixties, who hadn't visited a doctor in thirty years. He was a real cowboy, working his small ranch during daylight and dealing blackjack in the local casino at night. He believed I was a great doctor ever since our first meeting. Why? Because I'd taken time to listen to his concerns about not wanting to have a stroke. His brothers and father had all suffered recent strokes, which had been the impetus for him breaking his thirty-year hiatus from health care. He had no desire to live alone and disabled if he suffered a stroke. More than anything else, the fact that I'd listened and understood that real concern of his, was why he chose me to become his doctor—chalk up a few points to the art of medicine teaching us to listen to our patients.

At our first meeting, I discovered Don had high blood pressure but was otherwise in good health. He mentioned that he often dealt with some mild nasal congestion, and I gave him some samples of allergy pills. The pills worked wonders and that was it, he decreed I was brilliant and decided to come and see me throughout my residency, driving several hours from a neighboring state to visit.

He showed up to check his blood pressure and would spend 95% of our visit telling me stories about his female friend, "the judge," or about some girls that he had hit on at his blackjack table. I listened to his jokes (they were usually good), listened to his lungs (also good) and told him to see me again in six months.

One day however, he decided to change our familiar routine and asked me to look at some "spots" on his back and face. He was concerned because they'd been growing over the last year. I examined the spots and thought they looked only mildly concerning for skin cancer. I explained we could either biopsy them or just take them off. He had no concerns about scarring and preferred to just cut them out completely. Which was exactly what I preferred too.

Selfishly, I liked performing procedures in the clinic because I could block out large chunks of time and, in this case, sit and cut out his moles instead of listening to complaints from patients far less entertaining than Don.

When Don returned a week later for the mole removal, I had only been scheduled twenty minutes to remove three moles instead of the hour I'd requested. He had one mole near his eye, (normally a job for a plastic surgeon but, as mentioned, Don had no qualms about scarring) and two large ones on his back. If the whole procedure went well, I might just finish up within thirty minutes.

The procedure room was especially warm that day and the heat only increased when we turned on the large overhanging procedure light—the kind that looked like it's used for CIA interrogations. Also crowding into the small room were the nurse and a physician's assistant (PA) student who was interested in learning how to properly remove moles. I compliment myself on very few things, especially anything medical, but as mentioned above, I prided myself on being decent at suturing (thanks to good teaching, nothing innate). I was therefore happy to pass my fine skills on to the eager PA student. I should have been equally aware that pride in my medical abilities usually led to humbling experiences.

I explained my plan to Don and the student: I'd cut a wide resection around the awkwardly placed mole on his face, making sure the incisions aligned with the natural lines of tension. Your skin naturally pulls open one direction on your face based on the musculature beneath the skin, so you want to cut parallel with those lines, not perpendicular, which would increase the pressure to open the wound. I would instruct the student in proper suture technique as I worked.

The mole was either bigger than I remembered or had taken on a life of its own and grown significantly since the previous week. Either way, I was going to have to cut out a rather large elliptical piece of Don's forehead adjacent to his eye.

I kept asking Don how he was doing under the paper drape, lying there with his shirt off so I could wash the area properly without soaking his clothes. I cleaned the area around the mole, numbed the skin by injecting some local anesthetic, and proceeded to slice into Don's weathered face.

By now the room temperature was at a low broil. I could see

sweat forming under my latex gloves. Perspiration was pooling under my shirt. I used the scalpel to cut out the ellipse-shaped skin around the mole. A little blood oozed down the side of Don's neck, but luckily his shirt was off. All was going well despite the blistering room temperature.

I was about to complain that the room was a bit warm, and that Don might dehydrate like fruit under the drape, when somebody banged on the door and shouted, "Your next patient is waiting!"

Well stop scheduling them so close together, I thought, but replied, "Thank you… just a few more minutes."

I then proceeded to slice through a small artery on Don's forehead.

I knew it was an artery because the trickles of blood that accompanied the small incisions earlier in the procedure were remarkably different from the pulsating blood now spurting six feet across the room onto the clinic's white walls.

Why in the name of sweaty hot freaking overbooked clinic days are medical clinic walls painted white? It makes it really hard to cover up artery-slicing mistakes.

"Don, we might have to take care of the moles on your back next week," I calmly told him as I put some pressure on the open cut.

"Hey Doc?"

"Yes?"

"I think something wet just hit my chest."

"Oh yeah?" I said, admiring the pattern of blood splattered across his exposed torso.

"Everything OK?" He asked.

"Oh yes, just some bleeding. No problem."

It was times like these when I experienced momentary lapses in medical knowledge and wondered if perhaps, I had no idea what I was doing. *Perchance, had I forgotten some crucial anatomy rule about never cutting near this area on the face?*

I also began to wonder if Don would ever stop bleeding.

Perhaps he was doomed to bleed to death in front of us on this table? It seemed pretty likely at this point. I became convinced that if Don didn't die, I had probably cut an essential facial nerve and Don would never be able to shut his eye again.

Now, I'd closed wounds in a similar place in the ER. I previously described treating an eighty-two-year-old basketball fan with a cut on her forehead. She had wanted to stay for the game, despite blood spurting from her forehead onto other fans seated in front of her. She'd been dragged from the playoff game by paramedics and taken to the ER where I repaired the lacerated artery in the exact same place where I was making a mess of Don. But I couldn't remember anything at that moment, let alone the very dedicated eighty-year-old bloodied hoops fan.

The PA student looked at me, unsure if this fountain of blood was expected.

"Lots of vasculature up here," I reassured her with a smile. I continued to apply pressure and hoped that when I let go the wound would have stopped bleeding.

I peeked under the gauze and...no, no such luck whatsoever.

As the temperature rose due to four people being crammed into the small room with interrogation lights that highlighted the sweat now running down my face and threatening to drop onto Don along with his own pulsing blood, I initiated Plan B. Plan B was for the nurse to wipe the sweat from my brow. We then moved to Plan C. Plan C involved the PA student putting pressure on the wound while I would, as quickly as possible, suture some knots through the tissue surrounding the artery under the skin, then close the skin on Don's face with more sutures, and go see the irked patient waiting in a different exam room.

Plan C appeared to be working well as I was able to stop the artery from bleeding with one suture. Then I started to tie the first suture in his skin and *SNAP*! Not as in, "*Oh, snap!*" the crazy expletive used by Mormon lads in these parts, but, *SNAP*, as in the suture broke. Between the snap, my staring confusedly at the broken suture, Don starting to bleed again and someone turning the lamp to scald mode, the room temperature hit Swedish sauna levels.

For some reason, our clinic, of all the surrounding hospitals and clinics, had purchased cheap imitation suture that broke when any tension was applied. I had been well educated in proper suturing technique and knew very well that, when suturing a person's face, it was acceptable to use more than the usual quantity of sutures to help minimize scarring because you were only going to leave the finer 6.0 suture material in the skin for five days to avoid the tattoo marks of sutures. But you never wanted too much tension (i.e. to pull the sutures tight), it damaged the skin by cutting off blood flow. The suture should be delicately placed to approximate the wound edges together, but without pulling tightly.

At this overheated juncture however, I didn't give a shit about tension. I needed some baling wire and duct tape to close the damn thing up.

As I attempted to close the wound, yet again, the now annoying nurse banged on the door, "You have three patients waiting."

"Great, thank you." I replied, my voice starting to grate. "Don, going to have to finish your back next week. How are you doing under there?"

"Oh fine. *You* OK, Doc?" He asked, concerned for my wellbeing.

I went to work on the suturing and twenty minutes, twenty sutures, and countless boxes of cheap broken suture material later, we were finished. It actually looked good. Don walked out and I tried to ignore the blood splattered on his upper body, his pants, and the wall, certain I would never see him again after my barber-surgeon hackneyed efforts.

I then sauntered out to see the patients that had been waiting impatiently for forty minutes. Before I reached the designated exam room, however, I was halted by a fracas. In a room on my right, I saw an obese, middle-aged, sandy-haired patient slumped over in a chair, unconscious. Nurses and residents were trying to start an IV line and place EKG leads on her while figuring out why she'd suddenly passed out.

Fracases are uncommon in a clinic, so I asked another third-year resident if they needed any help and he shook his head, explaining, "I was kind of worried, but when we were placing the IV, she slyly opened her eyes to peek at what we were doing. She's fine." This was the kind of nonsense that patients, adults, no less, would go through to get attention in the hospital, ER, and clinics.

Even more remarkable, at least to me, Don showed up five days later to have both the sutures in his face and the moles on his back removed. He had not, for God knows what reason, lost faith in my brilliance after all. However, after what follows, I believe he must've reconsidered that decision.

Once more Don and the PA student joined me in a small room with inadequate space, no ventilation, and an interrogation lamp set to astral-scald temperature.

The moles on Don's back would be easy to remove compared to the delicate work his face had demanded. Once more I prepped the area around the moles, and cut away a large elliptical area of flesh, not quite a pound, but enough to feel a *Merchant of Venice*-like bond between us. Then it was time to piece Don back together again.

The wounds on his back, the ones I was responsible for creating, were huge—perhaps, on too late a second glance, too huge. As stated in the previous paragraph, removing them was easy, but now I had to close them up.

I started by pulling hard to bring the wound edges within shouting distance of each other.

SNAP!

The suture material broke. Try again…same result.

The first three sutures broke.

Shit, I thought, most possibly out loud, as I broke the fourth suture—I was now convinced that I had cut away too much skin

186

and would never be able to stitch the wounds together again. I began to ponder how embarrassing it was going to be to emergently send Don to plastic surgery for skin grafting.

Despite the light blaring down, the perspiration building on my brow, the PA student looking quizzical, and a nurse outside once again knocking to tell me patients were already getting tired of waiting, I managed to take a deep breath and started placing suture after suture in the wound, slowly pulling the edges closer together, not all the way, but closer—then I placed more and more sutures in between those first looser ones, until finally the skin on his back was pulled together with a mess of knots.

Don looked at the sweaty, fatigued, and frustrated image of his doctor under the lamp and asked, "Doc, *you sure you're OK?*"

He did not return for several weeks, and I was certain I had done some irreparable harm that had sent Don to the ER. He was most likely receiving an emergency skin graft. He had finally seen through the false image of me as a qualified doctor, seen me for the imposter I felt for all these years and undoubtedly, I should be expecting a lawsuit where I would stand in front of his lady friend, the judge, and be executed.

But weeks later Don returned and apologized for not showing up sooner; he'd asked a doctor in his hometown to look at the wounds and apparently, they'd been doing fine.

"Don, I thought you were upset and never coming back."

"Why would I do that? You're my doc, *geez!*" He replied and lay down to have the stitches removed.

It turned out the wound looked healthy, and the surrounding skin had healed perfectly as well. That was the last time I saw Don, as my residency ended shortly thereafter. I did make sure to recommend he continue his care with one of the new female residents that were going to be starting in the clinic after me—he needed some draw besides my brilliant medical mind to keep him showing up for his medical visits.

FLASH-FORWARD URGENT CARE WORK POST-RESIDENCY

AS PROMISED EARLIER, A SUTURING STORY FROM YEARS LATER:

My suturing work on Don was good practice for what lay ahead in my future, working as an urgent care doctor. One of my finest moments, of which no before and after photos exist to provide bragging rights, involved a complex and messy laceration on a construction worker after he crashed several floors down a building, battering through concrete rubble and scaffolding with his face.

When this torn, bloodied, swollen head on a body was escorted into the urgent care clinic, I immediately told the nurse he needed emergent transport to the hospital and to alert them to call their plastic surgeon. But this undocumented worker, without insurance, without much money, refused to go to the hospital. The patient's face and mouth were so damaged that he could not talk, so his friend begged me to try and repair what I could as they couldn't afford to go to the hospital for what I deemed appropriate care.

I couldn't tell what, in the mess of his face, were the remains of his lips, teeth, gums, tongue, or cheek, between jagged tears, debris, swelling, and blood.

I declined treating him several times, knowing that he absolutely needed a plastics team to repair his face. But they adamantly refused to go and pleaded so sincerely that they could not afford a hospital. So, I relented.

Hours later, after carefully removing all sorts of splinters, concrete, and debris from his soft tissue, and slowly figuring out what went where, I pieced the inside and outside of his lower face

188

together. I sent him home very swollen and with prescriptions for antibiotics.

Unbelievably, when he returned to be checked over the next days, he looked decent, and when he returned to have the sutures removed, he looked completely normal—no scar tissue, and somehow his lips, face, and nose all lined up correctly on his face. I was utterly amazed. That was probably the only time I wish there was a before and after photo of my suture work.

The nurses were impressed by the outcome, which always made me feel good. I think I told the front desk to charge him $200 for the entire treatment, which made the patient feel good. And for a fleeting few seconds, my medical imposter syndrome took a back seat to my feeling good about my patient care.

Flashback over, we now return to my regularly scheduled fumbling through the world of medicine.

THE RETURN OF THE CHIEF
RESIDENT

JACK & JOSEPH ON THE HIGH SEAS OF
EMOTION

We were in the final months of residency training and once more I was ordered back to the hospital front lines to work as the mole—the nighttime and weekend chief resident. My very first stint as the mole had been my very first minute as a senior resident. A bit overwhelmed, and a lot humbled on that first night. Now, many months later and close to graduating, I expected to oversee the inpatient service with a bit more poise and confidence than I had exhibited all those months ago.

I walked back into the hospital on my first night back as the mole, hesitating at the building's side entrance for one final glance back towards the sunset gilding the nearby foothills. I took a moment and breathed in the view. A brief rainstorm had just passed through, and several rainbows framed the green and gold hillsides I knew so well from trail running. Beautiful.

I left the serenity of the sunset and walked into the chaos of an incandescently lit hospital where several patients were already waiting to be admitted to the hospital floors from the ER.

My immediate concern at this hour was not re-orienting

myself to the hospital setting, was not meeting the twenty-three patients under my team's care for the night, was not checking the ICU patients to make sure they were breathing, was not even admitting the waiting patients. My concern was eating a proper dinner because the San Diego marathon was only one month away, and I needed to stay nourished and healthy as I had set a personal best goal in the marathon. So, with selfish priorities in order, I headed to the cafeteria before it closed.

The hallway from the resident's call room to the hospital cafeteria passes right through the labor and delivery ward. As I headed off to explore my dining options, dreaming of the culinary travesty awaiting me, I was intercepted by a nurse informing me that one of my friends was currently in labor. Surely this was some random clinic patient attempting to garner an extra hospital meal by carelessly tossing my name around in a familiar manner—just kidding, tossing my name around a hospital would be met with confused stares or a kick out the front door. But when I went to check on the patient, I discovered it actually was a very close friend of mine. I immediately entered their room to see how she and her husband were doing.

Her husband was doing just fine.

My laboring friend, however, was not very comfortable; it was her first baby, and her current early labor pain was excruciating. She had hoped for a natural childbirth but was now very willing to discuss the risks and benefits of receiving an epidural.

Early in her pregnancy we'd discussed my being her OB doctor. After thinking it over they'd opted for an OB not so intimately connected with them—which was great with me, as it relieved the pressure that I would somehow screw up her pregnancy. I was very close with this couple. Typically we would get together for bike rides or dinners when schedules allowed. The woman was someone I could pour my heart out to and receive her blunt mockery of my flailing social life in return. Given how close we were, it was a bit of a relief not to be in charge of her and her baby's wellbeing.

However, with her now in pain, they wanted my advice on how to proceed. I went to the nurse's station to check which resident was covering the labor and delivery deck that evening and decided it was best that I watch over everything rather than trust their care to this particular junior resident.

After double-checking that my friends did indeed want me medically involved (emotions were high, so I wanted them to be fully on-board with my participation), I ordered her epidural. Despite my preference to be a doctor on TV, I did enjoy—and did a good job— taking care of labor and delivery patients.

Then, while she was having her epidural placed, I ran upstairs to the fourth-floor to check on one of the newly admitted patients who was complaining of chest pain.

When I returned to check on my friend, she was slightly more comfortable, so I relaxed and headed back up to the fourth floor. I needed to make sure all the new patients being admitted had the proper orders written.

Before arriving in the hospital that evening, I'd received a message from my mother that I hadn't yet returned, and I now received a second one. I called her back. My grandfather had taken a sudden turn for the worse in his long-standing battle with prostate cancer and the awful side effects of chemotherapy. My grandmother, ninety-two years old at the time, with terrible osteo-porosis, had been doing her best to take care of him, but he was so sick that my aunt had gone to help out with his care. I had delayed flying out to see him myself because he'd supposedly been doing much better after his last round of chemotherapy. I would have time to see him after the busy weeks of being the mole ended. I hadn't seen him in years—engaged with this medical school and residency stuff and taking care of people.

Meanwhile, the night was becoming busier in the hospital: I had several more patients to admit from the ER, two sick people in the ICU needing evaluation, and nurses asking me about medicine changes that the interns should have taken care of but hadn't because they had 327 other things to do.

I was busy talking with a sickly eighty-nine-year-old woman we'd just admitted to a room on the fourth floor when my mother paged me yet again. The patient, scared of being alone in the hospital, was the same age as my grandfather.

My mother let me know that my grandfather was now unconscious, and she was going to fly to be with him. I hung up with my mother and went back to see the scared patient, re-assuring her that we would take good care of her overnight until her family returned the next morning.

Then my pager buzzed again. I looked down to check the new number. It was my mother, again.

I had no doubt the reason why she would page me back so soon. I went to the far side of the crowded nurse's station and called my mother. She tearfully confirmed what I'd already guessed; my grandfather had just died.

He was cynical and intelligent, and it was easy to imagine how tough it must have been for my mother growing up under his care. But I also knew he loved us all. He had been the first of my family to support my decision to follow whatever made me happy in my career choice, even if that meant leaving medicine. Once, only once, did I ever see him anything but serious, and this was when he was already in his eighties. He stood up from a kitchen chair and showed me how to dance to Hungarian Gypsy violins—he stood shuffling his feet and actually smiled. He'd eloped with my grandmother after leaving war-torn Europe. His last words were to her, his wife of sixty-three years, "I love you." Smiling to music and loving his wife is how I choose to remember him.

The hospital was slammed, and I had a mountain of work to complete. But I turned my chair towards the window for a minute, hung my head and wiped away the tears in my eyes. Then I told myself to get back to work and did so. I witnessed and comforted people going through this moment all the time, but it was always different when it was personal.

I had several patients needing to be seen on this hectic, and now painful night, so I quickly picked myself up and checked once more on the scared woman who was the same age as my now deceased grandfather before heading to the ER to admit the next patient.

As I headed back downstairs to the ER, I stopped back to see my friend in labor and delivery. Despite the epidural, her pain had actually worsened. I offered to become more involved with her care if she wanted, as nobody had been able to contact her OB doctor just yet. At this point, writhing in pain, she was more or less willing to agree to anything that might help. So I took over the role that we'd once agreed would be best to hand-off.

And there I was doing a pelvic exam on one of my closest friends to see what her baby was doing (besides choosing to stay warm and comfortable inside his mother). Her cervix was dilated but the baby was not yet descending as much as would be expected.

As I studied their baby's heart tracings on the monitor, I witnessed a few concerning patterns. Specifically, the heart rate was dropping during the contractions, which was normal, but not recovering as quickly as was expected—not troubling enough to immediately rush for a C-section, but enough for me to stay right there on the deck and watch closely.

This was an awkward situation because I didn't want to alarm my friends, as most likely everything would be just fine—but at the same time, given these people were like family to me, the idea of anything possibly going wrong was so completely anathema that I felt a wave of nausea flow over me. They had gone through an agonizing few years trying to become pregnant, and I wasn't going to be at all cavalier with the situation now.

We discussed what was happening and I explained that I wanted to put some monitors on the baby's head and inside her uterus to more accurately gauge how the baby was doing and to monitor if the contractions were strong enough to push the baby out. I screwed a monitor onto the infant's head and placed another line inside my friend's uterus, recognizing that husband and wife were now slightly concerned about my own heightened level of interest. So, I kept smiling and telling them we were just being cautious, and that everything would be fine.

Hours later the labor still hadn't progressed, and she continued to experience high pain despite the epidural—which the anesthesiologist had checked repeatedly. I would've been cursing out the earth itself had I been experiencing the nauseating, sweat-inducing waves of pain she appeared to be going through. It was time to talk about a possible caesarian section, which I knew she would not want, but the baby's heart rate had started going dangerously lower and there was no way I wanted to wait much longer.

All the worst possible scenarios run through your head when faced with treating close friends and family. The first time another close friend had asked me to take a look at her husband, who'd come home sick from work with a simple head cold, I'd given all the proper advice for how to treat the flu-like illness. Then I spent the entire night lying awake, convinced I'd missed a diagnosis of meningitis. I called and woke them up first thing the next morning to make sure he was still alive and to ask a host of questions related to meningitis. He was fine, nursing a cold, and quite annoyed that I had woken him up.

So now, not wanting to risk anything, I brought up the likelihood of needing a C-section before anything got worse for the baby. Maybe it was the threat of a possible C-section, but suddenly, after those words, that stubborn little guy decided it was time to enter the world and just like that, everything took a turn for the better and his majesty the baby was born.

The parents were both crying while I stood at the warming area with baby Jack, who wasn't crying too well and needed meconium (baby poop) sucked from his airway. Outwardly I was smiling, but my mind was freaking out, willing him to take a few deep breaths. We kept drying him off, rubbing him with blankets to stimulate him to warm up and breathe. I listened to his heart rate, which was still not fast enough; he wasn't breathing too strongly, and he looked pale.

My mind raced with everything we could possibly do—there was no way anything untoward could happen to this guy. Then, all by himself, he started to breathe just fine. Granted, he took his own sweet time, stressing me out over what felt like an hour, but there he was in his parent's arms, pink and crying. A gorgeous circle of life… and I still hadn't had time to eat.

Fortunately the rest of the month didn't compare to that night on the high seas of rolling emotions. Of most interest during the rest of the month, I auditioned for a commercial and remarkably got the part. I would be working overnight at the hospital as the mole before being relieved of duty at eight a.m. My call time for filming was at nine a.m. and the location was just under an hour away from the hospital—perfect, provided I didn't get called to the ER at 7:45 a.m. to admit any new patients.

As I should've expected, after I spent a busy night awake, the ER called me at six a.m. to admit a patient. I rushed through the admission and went back to my call room to stare at the clock. Three minutes later, at seven a.m., I received another call to admit yet another patient from the ER—and I needed to be gone by eight.

Those might've been some of my most rapid hospital admissions ever: "So you've got chest pain? Great. Let me listen to your heart." *Still ticking.* "OK, the intern will take care of you from here."

Fifty-eight minutes later I was in a film production trailer, not having slept for over twenty-four hours, swilling copious amounts of coffee, having make-up applied to keep the circles under my eyes from showing.

It was a commercial parody of the movie, *Deliverance*. A woman (who was an absolutely hysterical actor) and I played a yuppie couple out camping with our portable solar port that allowed us to recharge our laptop, electric toothbrush, etc. While we were calling to have massages and pedicures scheduled, two guys looking to be direct from the parodied movie run up and make me stand against my truck. Just when it looked like I was about to be violated and asked to squeal, they instead steal the electric toothbrush from my back pocket and run off laughing.

Sound silly? It was the number one web commercial in the world for some period of time (Hours? Months? Weeks? I don't know); it was eventually pulled because the volume of people watching was clogging the company's Internet server (this was many years ago and servers might have been less able to handle any significant volume). And then it was 5:30 p.m. and I turned into the hospital mole ready to stay awake for the entire night yet again.

That was the first time the interns had experienced me completely jacked up on caffeine and found it quite entertaining. I usually saw no reason to waste the effects of coffee at the hospital, where being grumpy did not seem out of place with the rest of the people working there. I had also abstained from coffee and doughnuts for almost eighteen weeks as part of my training plan for the San Diego marathon, so the effects seemed to hit me harder. The marathon was getting closer and so was the end of residency. I felt unprepared for either event.

Fortunately, the night provided some mild entertainment to keep my mind off the missed doughnuts and zero sleep.

To keep our program solvent, the residency had been forced to hire several new residents to make up for the three interns who'd transferred away midway through their intern year—the three interns I had ruled over as chief resident, who felt emboldened to follow their true medical calling. As you might suspect, there was a significant dearth of medical residents hanging around with nothing to do halfway through a residency year, hoping to transfer into our program. But we dredged several from the streets, which should have been warning enough, and one night I had the absolute cultural joy of working with a new Russian female resident.

I was shocked to discover she bore absolutely no resemblance whatsoever to the female Russian spy in the James Bond film, *The Spy Who Loved Me.* Even more demoralizing was her complete lack of ability to sense personal space. Wherever we walked, she angled her stride towards me, bumping into me as we walked shoulder to shoulder down an absolutely straight hallway. Maybe it was due to all that Chernobyl radiation leakage. Is there a word for this disorder where people walk into you as you supposedly stroll together in the same direction?

It became somewhat comical walking down the hall towards the ER, as she would start heading me off into a wall. Initially, I thought she was trying to hurt me, not that you could do a lot of damage running somebody off the hallway carpet, but still, I questioned her intentions. This inability to walk a straight line turned out to be the least of our problems.

We arrived in the ER to admit our first patient together, a sweet old man with cellulitis (a skin infection)—pretty much the single most straightforward case we admit for treatment.

Suddenly the new resident starts barking staccato Russian military-style interrogation questions at the confused patient: *"Do you have breath shortness?!"*

There was no reason to be concerned about "breath shortness" as he was doing just fine talking to us in full sentences. It was late and we needed to be efficient. I decided I would just take over the interview and help her out...

But before I could redirect her line of questioning back to anything relevant to the infection, she barked, *"Do other men sleep with you?!"*

I turned to stare at her, stunned, as she fired off yet another tangential question, "Do you have patters in the heart?"

What?

Hours later, after overseeing her bark irrelevant questions at our third patient of the night, wasting fifteen minutes on questions having nothing to do with why these patients were even being admitted to the hospital, I decided it would be much easier for me to not tell her about any new patients that arrived and do both our jobs in less time—although it was going to be confusing for her to explain who these new patients occupying beds were during morning rounds without me present.

After hearing subsequent accounts of her rounds, however, it may not have been any more confusing than her normal presentations after actually having seen the patients.

Also on the list of hospital blunders that night, somebody managed to order a tenfold-too- high dose of insulin for a twenty-six-year-old diabetic patient. Any lawyers want a slam dunk? Fortunately the patient survived and did well and, no, I had nothing to do with that patient order.

The next morning in clinic, having not slept in quite a long time and feeling extremely slaphappy, I met my most interesting patient of the day by far, and was willing to bet that few people had a similar conversation that day. She was a very genial woman with her wedding day rapidly approaching. She thought starting birth control would be appropriate with their honeymoon night ahead. She was quite nervous about "that night" and somehow, she chose me to write her a playbook and to describe what to do and what to expect.

And we were talking details, questions like, "Is my hymen still there and will intercourse hurt?"

"Yes, it's still intact and I guess it might hurt a bit when you have sex the first time as a woman...not that I know first-hand, but that's what I hear...but then it's supposed to get better."

"What if I can't fit him?"

Why are really silly answers the only thing coming into my head right now?

"Will I get aroused?"

Don't mothers cover this stuff? Or MTV? COSMO?

"What if he doesn't get aroused? What can I do that he would like? What do you like?"

Uh...

I gave up trying to keep a straight face and mumbled some unintelligible reply having nothing to do with her question. We both ended up laughing.

The next patient I saw in clinic that evening was a guy with a lot of back pain who I'd helped significantly by unwittingly feeding his drug-seeking desires with bigger and better narcotics over the last months. He swore that no other doctor had ever even believed his back pain was real. No other doctor was as empathetic as me (I had dealt with chronic back pain for most of my life—but never once took narcotic medications for it) and no other doctor was probably as stupid or naïve as me. He and his wife were in tears when I informed them that I was leaving the clinic soon, as my residency training was ending.

Later that evening my advisor informed me that the patient's oxycontin doses were similar to my prescribing heroin.

So, to recap my day: the Russians are body-checking me into hospital walls in an apparent attempt to avenge the 1980 Lake Placid loss (*Why me? I don't know*), I am sending little girls to bed forever traumatized with stories of what to expect on their honeymoon, and I deal heroin.

I want a raise.

EAR, NOSE & THROAT

AN EXHILARATING RUN. AN
UNDERWHELMING FINISH

My final month of residency (Huzzah!) started in San Diego. I had trained for the *San Diego Rock n'Roll Marathon* for eighteen weeks with long runs in snow and rain, interval training on a treadmill at night, and a decrease in hospital doughnut consumption. In fact, I had eaten well. I was rested. I was ready. And I knew any number of things could happen to thwart my sub-three-hour goal. Blisters. Sore back acting up. Upset stomach. But I really wanted to meet that goal, to run a marathon in under three hours.

During my intern year, I was completely unprepared for my first marathon due to a small pelvic fracture and spent the majority of the run dreaming of morphine and swearing I would never run a marathon again. The second year I showed up with several more training days under my belt, and it snowed the whole time. I was wearing shorts and didn't enjoy bordering on hypothermia the entire race.

Here I was in the last month of my third and final year of residency, and I'd trained well to meet my time. Someone described a marathon as a 20-mile warmup for a 6.2-mile race. And the first twenty miles went smoothly. Then, true to that perceptive marathon description, the last miles confirmed the theory of relativity, those miles lasted centuries longer than the previous twenty. I was exhausted. But as I closed in on the finish and saw the time clock reading 2:55, I asked people in the stands if that was really the finish? It was.

The race had little to do with medicine, but I will say this, that was probably my proudest moment during all the last years. I'm not sure what that says about my own self-worth regarding how medicine fit into my life. I did not feel much pride at the approaching graduation from residency, but that morning, sitting alone on a patch of grass past the finish line, I felt overwhelming joy at having achieved my goal.

I realize some metaphors could be painted between training for seven years to achieve a doctoring goal and working hard all those months for the marathon time goal. The difference I believe, which is good for those of you considering a path in medicine, is that if you put one foot in front of the other and follow the necessary path, then you will succeed in medicine. Running a marathon is a different type of challenge. Maybe the physical exhaustion contributes to high emotions, but just maybe, with so many variables which could make the race go wrong, despite all those days of waking extra early to run in sleet, twenty-mile runs in the rain, forgoing parties, eating well (I guess similarities might exist between the two endeavors), but when there is something you truly want, deeply desire, even if the stakes, in this case running a sub-three-hour-marathon, are self-imposed and valueless, well, not getting it seems a whole lot worse. This race goal was something I really wanted, and over the previous years, there had not been a lot of those moments.

Then I was back at the residency for a month of working with an Ear, Nose and Throat doctor (ENT). But after completing the marathon, everything else seemed relatively easy—maybe because I was back to eating doughnuts. We looked in people's noses and prescribed medicine for their nasally-inflamed allergies. We looked at scans of their sinuses and prescribed antibiotics for their chronic sinus infections. Far more interesting was watching nasal surgery. Just plain barbaric. Chopping, hammering and chiseling away until the patient's nose was swollen and black and blue.

The next best part was seeing the same patients return for follow-up visits. The ENT doctors would plunge deep into their victim's noses with pliers, then pull out the longest, largest pieces of snot imaginable, which gave the patients an addictive rush of ecstasy.

The last days of residency flew by. I missed graduation. I heard it was nice, but I had a good friend in town I hadn't seen in years. I'm sure there's some *Psych 101* issues that could be discussed here and I admit that after not feeling altogether wanted by the residency program over the last three years, I might have developed some subconscious issues that influenced my decision not to appear. Despite training in medicine for seven years, I still felt like I didn't belong. Imposter syndrome remained alive and well.

Then again, I had also missed most of my high school graduation—and given the chance, due to my divorced parents fighting, would gladly have missed my college one as well—but we had a wonderful speaker (Playwright John Guare), so I'm glad I made that one. And in *Playing Doctor; Book One*, you might've read how I arrived last minute, under threat of death, at my medical school graduation as everyone was walking inside. I'm just not a big fan of graduations. Bunch of pomp and sentimentality designed for the graduate's parents. I'll kill my kids if they miss graduation.

I finished my last days in my clinic, told all my patients I was leaving and received a horde of gifts—mostly home-made crafts from the patients in rehab centers and nursing homes.

I wrote a final e-mail from the clinic to my friends announcing that my time was done and that I was getting in a car and driving to the *Telluride Wine Festival*. The board exam was not for several weeks. It was time to celebrate.

I realize this might seem like a sudden end to medical training, but as you'll see, I was just getting started.

BOARD EXAMS & BREAKUPS

GET A JOB? ME? AS A DOCTOR??

July rolled around and the family practice board exam was only a couple of weeks away, but I wasn't too worried. I had studied for the LSAT's (law school entrance exams) with a pocketbook called, *"How to Cram for the LSATs in 5 days,"* and hoped the same publishers might have something similar for medical boards. Either way, I had a stress-free twelve days to study. That was until the woman I was dating thought it best for me to go home with her to Colorado for the 4th of July rather than studying for my medical board exams.

So I quickly cast the idea of studying aside and went to Colorado. First, Winston (my dog), vomited all over her car. Then, two days later, I proceeded to crash the same vehicle. I was not doing very much to make a good impression with this fantastic woman. She was a single mother who needed stability and responsibility and was quickly realizing that currently I lacked both virtues. That driving feat was not too impressive either, given I was in a driveway. Eventually I headed home and once again settled into the idea of studying.

A few days later I flew to L.A., where I was scheduled to take the exam. Modern medical board exams might take place on computers at every medical program, but back in those dark ages there were only several locations that hosted large contingents of recently graduated family practice residents to sit at desks with pencils and shade in circles in order to test and document your supposed doctor skills.

This L.A. journey seemed apropos: I had started my pre-med work on the East coast, moved west to the mountains for training, all along wanting to be in the film world and here I was taking the medical boards in La-La land itself. My mecca. The mecca I wanted to visit for totally different reasons, but there I was, in Hollywood (West Hollywood), completely understudied for my last round of boards.

I stayed with several of my girlfriend's close friends, one of whom was a celebrity hairdresser. I needed to get up early and drive out to some unknown location in this unfamiliar town renowned for traffic brawls, so a good night sleep was in order. Instead, much more in line with the rest of my training, I stayed up watching movies with my hosts until the wee hours of the morning, hoping one of the hairdresser's famous movie star customers would pop over for a drink, see me, and say I was perfect for a role in their upcoming movie.

Hours later, my disillusion shattered, I followed directions through L.A. and into the conference center of a large hotel with thousands of family practice residency graduates eager to slay their board exam. People were diligently studying on the floors, quizzing each other, talking about jobs, raving about extra rotations they had done in Africa.

Meanwhile, with my head on my desk, I tried to get some much-needed sleep and was instead forced to overhear conversations such as, "Remember *Robertson's Pathology Book of Diseases?* The photos of Leismaniasis? Remember? Remember the edema?"

"Yeah."

"I saw it."

"No!"

"Yeah. Full on."

"No!"

"Yeah!"

These people had apparently traveled to planet earth with the sole purpose of driving me insane. Their enthusiasm at this early hour was nauseating. Or maybe I was just tired because I had stayed up until 4 a.m. watching movies with a hairstylist to the stars.

The fellow next to me studied until the test administrators demanded, for the fourth time, that he put his book away, and then he kept studying with the book hidden under his desk while the usual No. 2 pencil announcements were delivered.

Even at lunch, while I sat outside on the curb reading Nick Hornby's *High Fidelity*, everybody around me either studied or went over their questions and answers from the first half of the day. Then we were invited back for a second round of in-depth multiple-choice guesswork.

That afternoon they took my test away and I was finished.

And there it was—I'd completed all aspects of my medical training and taken the board exams. I knew I didn't ace the exam, but I only needed to pass in order to get my medical license, and I felt confident I had done well enough to pass—not that I felt prepared to work as a doctor with or without that supposed stamp of validity.

Weeks later I received a letter stating I had passed. I'm not sure I even saw the score as I was pretty indifferent to medicine at this point. If anything, I should have been thrilled, but I was thirty-three years old, had a medical license and did not know what I was going to do with my life. But at long last, after seven years of having my schedule dictated to me, I could finally focus on what I wanted to do.

I finally had all the free time in the world to write all the movie scripts that had been percolating in my brain. And for the next several months I stared at a blank computer screen and could not come up with a single damn thing to write.

I BECAME A BIT DISHEARTENED. THEN, FED UP WITH MY SEEMING desire to not pursue a responsible career, the woman I'd dated for the last several months decided it was over between us. I didn't really appreciate her making such a decision without consulting me first, I was a doctor after all. She was wonderful and responsible and far more mature than me, and how could a single mom stay with a guy who did not know what he was doing with his life?

I went into a deep funk. I barely ate or slept for weeks. I went for long runs. I lost a lot of weight. I furiously scribbled long notes at 3 a.m. to myself in an indecipherable handwriting that bore a closer resemblance to Sanskrit than any modern written language.

I was alone with a medical degree and a mountain of debt. I became more depressed, which likely added to my not writing any of the screenplays I'd anticipated getting on the page. I could not afford to move to L.A.

Finally, I decided to consult some friends about my plight. The overwhelming consensus was that getting a job might be a good idea. This was a tough decision for me. I wanted that starving artist edge, but the bills were piling up, including my medical school loans being overdue, along with rent and credit cards bills. I also had no desire to starve, so I looked for a job.

I first went to the people I'd worked with for the past few years at the University Family Practice program, applying for a job as the family practice doctor at their Park City ski town clinic.

We sat down for what seemed like a friendly interview. Lo and behold the doctor interviewing me had my residency advisor's reviews in hand, which included my all too candid statements regarding my interest (or lack thereof) in medicine. For some unfathomable reason they asked about my comments regarding medicine not being my primary interest, and then commented that I did not seem too interested in pursuing medical work.

There you go, nitpicking again. I thought we had worn that path down, but apparently not, I was still persona non grata in the family practice world and was turned down for my honesty.

I finally found a job working a few nights a week in an urgent care facility, also operated by the University of Utah hospital. And this is probably a life lesson: just get in the game. After a few nights working in this clinic (and being paid!), the doctors I worked with realized I was hardworking and quite competent. They asked me to take more and more shifts. Within two weeks I had three offers from the exact same family practice people who had initially rejected me, offering me the choice of full-time positions at the Park City clinic, or two other University Family Practice clinics. I could choose where I wanted to work *AND*, they were willing to pay a significantly higher salary than the one I'd applied for and not received.

The offers (and validation) sounded nice. The dream ski town job in my sights with an increased pay scale. But during those weeks I'd spoken with some of the family practice doctors employed by the University and the words *overworked, stay late every night, not well supported, underpaid...*were used to describe the work situation. While I'd appreciated those same conditions as a medical resident, I decided to seek out some alternatives.

I instead signed up with a newly-opened, privately owned "Doc-in-the-Box" urgent care center where the owner had a crazy idea of keeping the staff and patients happy along with providing compassionate, high quality medical care.

Revolutionary.

Right up until he started making profits, got greedy, started forcing staff to provide negligent medical care in order to increase revenue, and then lied to me about profit-sharing and ownership —but that downturn was awhile away.

For several years that urgent care job provided some quality entertainment while working long hours with a great work staff. The shift type work also allowed me free time to act and produce several theater productions, to write film scripts, and to produce and direct one feature film, *Peloton* (rebranded as *The Cyclist* and available on Amazon).

Around the same time, I attended a yoga workshop that was being held in a strip-mall. This workshop was a graduation gift from my now ex-girlfriend. Being far more mature than me, she saw no reason for us not to travel to the workshop together. So, I grumpily sat in the backseat of her car plotting how to win her back, while some yoga guy sat in the front seat flirting with her.

In the workshop, I sat on my mat waiting for the class to start, far from my ex-girlfriend and the obnoxious fellow hitting on her with his yoga poses. Meanwhile, a woman had unrolled her mat next to me, the petulant grouch. This cheerful woman gave me a friendly greeting, laughing at my toes which were wrapped in duct tape to cover the blisters I'd gained while attempting to burn out my depression with long runs. I stammered some sort of reply and finally looked up at her, a radiant and smiling woman.

Little did any of us know where that yoga workshop meeting would lead. The world, unaware to me, the self-absorbed idiot, had just become far more wonderful and interesting.

See, that wasn't so bad: one year of post-baccalaureate pre-med classes, smile through four years of medical school and live in the hospital for three years of residency. Cakewalk. Just keep smiling and putting one foot in front of the other.

STRIP MALL URGENT CARE (THE ONE BEHIND ASTRO-BURGER)

WHERE I START MY CAREER IN PEDIATRIC NEUROSURGERY

My very first patient, on my very first night as a fully employed doctor at the urgent care clinic, was Conor, a two-year-old boy with a foreign body in his nose. The medical descriptor "foreign body" suggests that Paulina Porizkova was likely invading Conor's nasal passages. Or maybe a Scottish bagpipe troupe. Or perhaps Greek olives. The not-so-exotic foreign body was a popcorn kernel.

Foreign bodies find their way into kids' noses and ears with alarming frequency—a frustrating problem for parents and doctors alike—but I guarantee the kids abhor the resulting removal more than anyone. Popcorn kernels, marbles, foam from furniture kids pick apart, M&Ms, you name it—there is something intoxicatingly irresistible to certain kids about shoving objects up their noses or into their ears.

Adults find places to get objects stuck too, but with kids, it's typically ears and noses—often involving repeat offenders. But in this, my virgin case as a fully employed doctor, Conor was more or less innocent and the real instigator behind the ensuing debacle was Conor's older brother, Peter.

Peter, at the ripe age of four, was on a personal quest to crush world serenity. It was Peter who'd successfully encouraged Conor to stick the popcorn kernel up his nose in the first place. It was now up to me, the freshly minted physician, to christen the start of my new career by removing the invading kernel.

I entered the cramped exam room and assessed the situation: Conor was likely the crying and spasmodic toddler being wrangled down on the table by a woman I hoped was his mother. She was attempting to relax him using a gentle voice, "Conor, calm down, Conor, it's OK, he's a doctor and he's…Conor, you need to stop crying, Conor, he's a doctor, Conor, please…" Unsurprisingly, her efforts were not the slightest bit effective.

Good luck calming down a kid by telling them a doctor needs to do something. Any trust in doctors had been shattered by that kid's first round of pediatric immunizations.

Meanwhile, in the far corner of the room, Conor's grandmother held Conor's sleeping baby sister. But my focus was quickly drawn to the middle of the room where a whirling Tasmanian Devil repeatedly bellowed, "Connnnnorrrrr!!!!" This apparition turned out to be Peter, the aforementioned four-year-old, spinning at a dizzying velocity on my chair.

After quick introductions, and having my shoes untied twice by Peter, it was time to remove the kernel. Conor squirmed and wrestled as multiple nurses held him down, while I shone a light into his nose and saw the invading kernel reflecting brightly back at me.

I considered the options for extraction: a dab of superglue applied to the end of a swab was one option; but all I could envision was Conor moving around, the glue getting stuck inside his nose, then sending Conor to the ER with a medical swab glued to the inside of his nose and the kernel more firmly lodged inside. We didn't have a mini-suction device that could pull out the kernel. Instead, I would try to grasp the shiny, smooth object. I calmly inserted a long, thin set of pliers, deep into Conor's nasal passage.

At that point, right when the foreign body extraction was beginning to feel more like neurosurgery, Peter jumped on the exam table and knocked my arm, almost plunging the pliers deep into Conor's brain.

Conor's mother screamed, "PETER! STOP! STOP IT!"

Peter leapt off the table and began whooping his own name in a Celtic war cry, "Peter! Peter! Peter! PETEEEERRR!!" as he ran laps through the confined exam room, banging, continually, into all of us.

The grandmother, fed up with being run into several times, started yelling too, "Peter! Stop running! PETER! STOP IT!!"

The yelling did nothing to stop or slow Peter but did wake the baby sister, who opted to join in the festival of screaming.

At this point, being held down while the world around him went berserk, Conor realized (justifiably) that his mother's gentle reassurance that he needed this procedure was more likely an attempt to lobotomize him before he turned out like Peter.

So Conor started yelling as well, "No!No!No!No!No!No!NO!NO!NO!NO! NOOOOOO!!"

I honestly had no idea kids could make that much noise without taking a breath. I tried calming him down, suggesting a simpler technique to dislodge the kernel: "Connor, will you blow your nose?"

"No!"

"Will you sit still then?"

"No!"

"Then blow your nose."

"No!NO!NooooNonononononoooooo!"

Why he refused blowing his nose over the pliers in the head routine, I have no idea.

And then he started hyperventilating while snot and tears ran down his face. Total disaster.

His mother glared at me, as though the entire incident, from kernel insertion to family meltdown, was somehow my fault.

I looked around at the chaos and accepted defeat. I sent the entire family, most of them now bawling in tears, off to the children's hospital ER, where I figured the staff could sedate at least two, if not more, of the family.

I was 0-1 for the night (for my new job, actually), having fallen to a two-year-old.

I needed a boost and walked into the next patient room to examine a woman with a cough. Sounded simple. She took one look at me, pointed accusingly, and shouted, "You're a man!"

I looked around and realized I was the only other person present. "Yes, yes, I am," I replied. Quickly glancing at her chart, I discovered she was a paranoid schizophrenic patient living in some sort of mental rehab center.

She insisted she would only speak with a female physician. I was, however, the only doctor working. I explained this problem regarding her gender-specific desires several times before she relented and began discussing her cough, but she quickly saw through my guile.

"But you're a man!" she asserted yet again.

"You're right," I replied, once more validating her identification skills. "And remember, I'm the only doctor here. So will you tell me about your cough?"

"You're not a woman."

"No, I'm not."

"I want a woman doctor."

"Can you pretend I'm a woman doctor?"

"That's silly."

After ten more minutes of what I agreed was a silly conversation, I left the room and had a female nurse go ask the patient a list of questions I wrote down.

Meanwhile, I sat on the floor outside the room, my back to the wall, 0-2 for the night, unable to treat my second patient in a row.

Eventually, over the next hours, I actually treated some patients and over the following weeks slowly accepted my role as a doc-in-the-box. At any moment patients could walk inside the clinic with all sorts of injuries, complaints, diseases, or disorders, and I was the only doctor there to care for them.

I was scheduled to work several fourteen-hour shifts a week and had the rest of my days free to audition for acting roles and to pursue my writing. I was working at a fun (relatively speaking, compared to 120-hour work weeks in the hospital) job and gaining confidence in my medical abilities. The patients liked me, the staff liked me, and I was quickly promoted to Medical Director of the clinic. Charles Dickens might have written my tale.

Granted, I was a doctor in an urgent care clinic, the fast-food center of the medical world, taking care of patients' immediate needs, be it hunger, stroke, or a case of the sniffles—I was there to serve. The food service analogy was far more apt than you may believe.

There were moments I actually found myself saying, "Well, it seems you ordered the special of the night. It's sinusitis that simmered nasally for two weeks. And tonight you've won your choice of two antibiotics. May I suggest the Augmentin? It goes wonderfully with a decongestant."

After receiving a blank stare from patients, I regained kudos by asking, "You want a cough syrup with that?" This was simple medicine, caring for mostly simple people. If anything, the work provided me with a glimmer of hope that maybe I wasn't the simpleton I'd led myself to believe—or perhaps once again it was all relative as I was seeing many signs that as a civilization, we were not evolving quickly at all.

Late one night, as I counted down the final minutes to my four-teen-hour shift ending (I typically ended up being there for sixteen hours, so it was quite exciting to leave after fourteen), a young teenage boy was dragged inside by his father to have a BB removed. Most BB injuries resulted from hunting accidents, or from a friend shooting you in the ass as a joke in high school (my friend, my ass). And most patients came in immediately to have the invading pellet removed.

I walked into the procedure room to find a young Darwin-Award-candidate-in-the-making with an ugly wound right between his eyes. I had to ask how this messy and bloody injury had occurred. It turned out the injury was neither a hunting accident, nor a poorly aimed shot at his ass. No, this young buck had managed to shoot *himself* in the forehead. As interesting as the details in this incident might have proved, I feared it would open a Pandora's box of familial psychosocial issues that I had no desire to open at that late hour. So instead I asked when he'd shot himself, as the wound did appear quite fresh.

The BB shot had occurred neither today, nor yesterday, nor last week. He'd shot himself between the eyes several months ago. The surprising part about it occurring several months ago was that the wound was still bleeding. So I inquired why it looked like a new wound.

"Well, I tried to cut it out last night," the teen replied. I looked more closely and sure enough there were cut marks radiating out in every direction, making a big star right between his eyes.

Now, truly amazed, I stammered, "You tried to cut it out yourself? With what?"

"A scalpel."

I don't know, maybe scalpels are readily available these days and with the glut of medical television shows one might be inspired to perform surgical procedures at home. *But on yourself?* This fellow came from the same basic DNA stock as people who had produced power from wind, discussed quantum physics, and perhaps one day this young man's societal contribution would be in plastic surgery, but for now it was just stupid, and more importantly, keeping me at work later than I wanted. Perhaps the acorn had not fallen too far from the tree as I now learned about the dad's powers of observation.

The patient had walked out of his bedroom the previous night with his forehead gushing blood. Observing the bloody mess, the father considered that perhaps the three-month-old, large lump between his son's eyes was not a big zit after all. Piqued by the sight of blood, the father had then made his son confess to his self-serving surgical feats of mutilation.

Which brought us to the current evening, when he'd brought the unwilling patient into my clinic to allow a proper attempt at BB removal, to have the disfigured forehead put back together, and mostly, to prevent my going home at a decent hour.

Given that I was now going to be in clinic an extra hour, I took time to explain the inherent dangers in shooting oneself in the head.

My sober attitude seemed to confuse the father. "Well Doc, how come you're the only one not laughing?"

Because this is a mess and I have no desire to be here at this hour and why the hell did you wait until 10:01 to show up at our doorstep? We were here for the previous fourteen hours and on this, the one night I almost left at a decent hour, you show up, that's why I'm not laughing.

But I didn't say that.

This father was the same guy who was trying to convince me to do the procedure without anesthetic to teach his son a lesson. The son did indeed need a lesson. His last visit to the doctor had been for sutures after he cut himself in the head playing with a sword.

May I suggest revisiting first grade, where I believe they attempted to teach lessons in common sense?

The BB removal turned out to be more complicated than I suspected, because the BB, after waiting months for an exit visa, had buried itself deep inside scar tissue. Not to mention, a BB is a round slippery fellow. After finally removing the pesky bugger, I was then faced with repairing the skin that was sure to scar in a bizarre pattern on his forehead and likely be viewed as a satanic worshipping symbol. All things considered, it gave me a sense that while I may not be the sharpest tack in the box, I was not the dullest, either. Then again, after paying to be under-slept and intimidated for eight years, maybe a BB to the head didn't sound so bad after all.

Was I already becoming a cynical clinician in my first months?

IF CYNICISM WAS SNEAKING BACK INTO MY MEDICAL MINDSET, I think it fair to blame my favorite scapegoats, the patients. All my favorite types of patient cases from the years of training showed up for the exact same reasons and there were times, dealing with the nonsense, that it was absolutely draining.

One busy clinic afternoon, I watched Becky being brought back into a clinic room. Her first mistake was being super friendly. Several studies had shown that drug-seeking individuals were often quite pleasant, flattering you as the one and only caring doctor that ever helps them during their times of need.

As Becky walked past me in the clinic hallway, she jovially asked, "Hi, how are you doc? So great to see Julie [one of our staff] here today, we go way back. Guess I'll be seeing you soon." She then performed an exaggerated limp off stage into an exam room.

She might as well have waved a banner overhead declaring, "Me? I want narcotics!"

Julie then popped out from the reception desk to warn me, "A woman Becky is here. She thinks we're friends. I don't even know her. She's a narc seeker, just to let you know."

I looked over Becky's DOPL report (Department of Professional Licensing report) that shows doctors a list of all controlled substances prescribed to individuals. Becky had received Lortab prescriptions from thirteen different doctors in the previous three months—a very impressive haul.

When I walked into the exam room, Becky writhed in pain, bemoaning her woeful story:

"Oh doc, it's killing me. I had knee surgery a few weeks ago. Then my horse kicked my knee yesterday. I'm gonna kill that horse. I'm all bruised. It's horrible. Aaarrrgghh. Oh god, oh god, I need help with the pain."

At which point she showed me her knee that was indeed mildly swollen, and red with a tiny bruise off to one side.

When a horse kicks your knee, it typically shatters your kneecap; it seldom glances off with a warning bruise.

Becky continued her harrowing tale, concluding with the fact that her orthopedic doctor was out of town; otherwise, she would just have gone to see him for the injury.

Using keen, detective-like perception, I noted some well-healed surgery scars around her knee that fit with her story; as well as several fading (or washed off) black magic marker lines demarcating the redness at the top of her knee. The exact type of mark somebody in an ER would draw to follow the progression of a skin infection.

So I asked her, "Were you seen anywhere else recently, seen by some other doctors?"

"No."

"Nobody drew lines on your leg to mark the redness?"

"No."

"Nobody at an ER or urgent care drew those lines on your leg?" I asked, pointing to the black marks outlining the area of redness on her leg."

"Well, I went to a *different* ER last night, but they just thought I had a skin infection 'cause my skin was red. I told them the redness was just sunburn and they just gave me antibiotics. They wouldn't give me any pain medicine. I told them the redness was just a sunburn."

I asked her to show me her other knee for comparison. Her other leg and both arms were pasty white.

"Silly question, but how come you don't have a sunburn anywhere else?" I politely inquired with genuine curiosity.

"Well, my chest is really burnt," she replied, puffing it out for exhibit. At this point I glanced inquisitively at her distractingly low-cut shirt that displayed a healthy amount of alabaster white cleavage. Flirtatious female patients also trigger alarms for potential drug-seeking behavior.

She then repeated for the third time that her doctor was out of town otherwise she would have gone there for her pain medications. Yet one more warning sign: a patient asking you for pain medicine because their usual doctor is out of town—and this excuse always seemed silly to me in an age where telephones exist, because how difficult did patient's think it was for us to call their supposed doctor's office?

"Did you call his office and talk with the doctor on call?" I asked.

"No. They're all away at some conference."

I told Becky I needed to have the records faxed from the other ER to determine what medications they had used for her supposed infection.

My desire to know what medications she had been prescribed the previous night baffled Becky when all she needed was some pain medication. I explained that I would also attempt to call her doctor because if she had an infection from surgery, then she might require different antibiotics than the ones prescribed, and she likely needed an exam by her surgeon.

When I called her orthopedic surgeon's office, the clinic's nurse practitioner audibly groaned when I mentioned Becky's name. Before I said anything else, the nurse told me that Becky had called her four days ago, claiming that she had been kicked by a horse, and demanding pain medications. Becky had been told to come into the orthopedic clinic, but never showed up. The nurse also told me that Becky had a narcotic contract with the orthopedic doctor (narcotic contracts are signed agreements that the patient can *only* receive controlled substances from that one doctor) and had been told she needed to go into drug rehab. And yes, the doctor was both in town, and willing to see Becky immediately.

I returned to Becky and asked, "Were you kicked by a horse earlier in the week as well?

"No," she replied. "Why?"

"Because your doctor's nurse practitioner said you called her four days ago asking for pain medication because you were kicked by a horse. Do you think you have a problem?"

"Yeah, I have a problem. It's that I really don't like the doctor or the nurse there."

Well now the cards were on the table.

"Becky, I'm at a loss here. You have this confusing story of surgery, being kicked by a horse, twice in one week, sunburn on one limb that looks more like an infection, and a story of your doctor being out of town when he's not. I can't really figure out what's going on, but your doctor is waiting to see you today."

"Oh." long pause with blank stare, "So, can you give me some Lortab until I get there?"

I swear to God I would like to sue all the narcotic abusers for restitution of the wasted time that I will never get back.

OVER THE NEXT WEEKS, I BEGAN TO FEEL THAT MY MEDICAL CAREER was analogous to my doctor role in the doomed TV pilot audition in this books prologue – by appearance, my career was weighty and purposeful, but in reality, it was full of nonsense and guess-work, and difficult to take too seriously.

For example, one patient came into the clinic after she'd been making potato salad, and like most women in this conservative town, was doing so naked. Hold questions please, things do get more complicated. She slipped and landed on a potato, which, as potatoes have a preternatural habit of doing, had become lodged in her vagina.

My fellow doctor saw her that day and apparently the line, "There's no potato, we've lost the salad," would have been appropriate. I can imagine certain minds out there pondering this situation, and the answer is, I don't know what kind of potato.

That incident happened only days after a different woman had come into the clinic complaining to me that, "Something fell out of my vagina."

"Well, let's not beat around the bush, what was it?" I asked. Baffled by my interrogation techniques, she shrugged her shoulders, confused. I kept thinking, *she must have a clue*; this cannot be a complete mystery. But she swore she did not know.

I wanted to play charades, "Animal, vegetable, or mineral? Sounds like?"

Despite doing a thorough pelvic exam, I never discovered whatever it was that might have so inexplicably fallen.

The reality of my current life as a doctor was dealing with randy russets ("Potatoe," Mr. Vice President? (*An ancient reference to Vice President Quayle notoriously telling an elementary school boy who had correctly spelled the word "potato" that he needed to add an "e" onto the word.*) and vaginal enigmas, while I attempted to persuade non-medical people that I was able to accurately administer CPR to furniture during my free time in television auditions.

How seriously could I take my life or position as a physician? In fact, I felt I was starting to resemble that line in the doctor role audition that opened this book, *"There's no pulse, we've lost him."*

Perhaps it was due to the sudden realization that I actually had a job, but I began to ask myself the question, *what am I doing?* Why was I working in the field of medicine in the first place? Was dealing with these patient's gobbledygook really to be my life's work? I was trying to accustom myself to being a "Doc-in-the-box," accepting that it was a perfect role for me, with its flexible schedule, decent enough pay for my simple life, and enjoyable work that allowed me to pursue other goals. But really, what the hell was I doing working in a strip mall behind *Astro-Burger*?

Then, at just the right time, I was invited to Telluride for my friend Dave's surprise fortieth birthday party.

INTERMISSION IN SEARCH OF INSPIRATION

ESCAPE TO TELLURIDE

Telluride had always been a place to find some clarity and to celebrate (clarity and celebration often appearing in tandem at a bar over clinked glasses) and this weekend was to be no exception. It was my time working at the Telluride Medical Clinic that had convinced me to apply to family practice residency programs in the first place. Jump now to Friday evening, where the sun's rays were still hitting the town and glowing on the mountainside. It was beautiful outside, with blue skies, and I had thirty minutes before I was due for cocktails at the Opera house—what's not to love?

Plenty of time to grab some coffee and relax in the setting sunlight while I contemplated my life's queries: Why did I become a doctor? Was I happy in my strip mall job? Should I buy new ski gear? Why was the thirty-nine-dollar portable CD player acting up on the drive down to Telluride? What should I wear to the next night's surprise party? But for some odd reason I decided to stop by the medical clinic and say hello to my old friends working there and quell any rumors that I was now working as a goat herder.

Inside the clinic I swapped stories with the nurses working and they shared the latest gossip. The last person I asked about was the clinic director. She was the doctor I'd been the least close with after all my time working there intermittently, starting in medical school—mostly because I held a grudge that she'd made me write health-related articles for the local newspaper. That said, she was a very nice woman; both she and her husband spent time skiing, hiking, climbing, and biking and were very civically oriented, being very active in town affairs—although I must admit I'd always found her psychiatrist husband a bit arrogant.

The nurses then told me that several months earlier, her husband had bicycled out to go rock climbing. He never returned home.

The Search and Rescue team found him by the river, unsure of anything that had happened that day. I'll spare you the details, but he was taken to MD Anderson Medical Center in Houston and diagnosed with a brain tumor. It turned out to be the worst kind possible. They had cut the tumor out, zapped him with radiation, administered chemotherapy, and the damn thing kept growing. So the clinic director was taking time away from work until the end, as in his final chapter. Then one of the nurses told me that they loved receiving visitors. And I felt I was expected to go say hello.

I left the clinic and headed back into town. What I really wanted was my coffee and to relax until the designated cocktail hour; but I started walking up the hill towards their house.

The hill was steep, and I couldn't exactly remember where to find their house. And again, I kind of just wanted to head back to town rather than sit with the clinic director and her arrogant, dying husband who didn't really know me, anyway.

It's uncomfortable to sit with people in those grieving situations; there was not much to say, all you could do was be present with them, let them know you cared and empathize with their pain and grief. It was depressing, it was sad, it was painful, and I would rather be laughing inside a bar.

As I trudged up the hill, all sorts of lame reasons to not go kept popping into my head: The bar might get busy, and I would have to wait for my gin and tonic. They might keep talking and talking and I would miss cocktails altogether.

But I felt compelled to keep walking up and to find their house, which I eventually recognized due to the hastily constructed banister on the outside steps with neon orange tape marking all the step's edges. The design of both was obviously to help an unsteady person balance on the stairs. There was a single light on inside the house and I could see somebody sitting hunched over a desk.

I knocked on the front door. The director's conceited husband stood up from the desk and opened the door to greet me.

The entire right half of his head was shaved, displaying a large scar in the shape of an "S." The other half of his head looked like a skunk having a God-awful hair day, with tufts of hair sticking out in every direction. His balance was shaky, and he teetered while standing, but he shook my hand with a ton of strength and energy.

I told him that I'd heard about what had happened and just wanted to stop in and say "Hello."

This was his reply as he balanced precariously: "Thank you so much for coming up here! Well, I am doing great, really good, I mean, it got gritty there for a while, but now we're doing really great...I am so lucky to have my wife, I just love her...And I feel so bad because she has the weight of the world on her right now, but we're doing really good, really, really great...."

Then he asked me my name again and this time I told him that his wife would know me as Johnny Utah. Upon hearing my old town pseudo-name, he got really excited, saying that now he remembered me and that his wife would be so sad to have missed me.

And that was it.

I walked out of that house, down the stairs marked with orange neon tape, into the setting sun gilding the street back to town.

And the thought hit me, *well that just changed my life.* Here was a guy standing toe to toe with death, no more skiing, no more climbing, no more walking to town for coffee—and more importantly, maybe just a few more months, weeks, or even days left with his wife; days left to shake hands with people stopping by, and he knew that, and he had the goddamn courage to stand there and to tell me how great he was doing.

Well damn it, at that point how can you do anything but recognize just how great your own life is? I celebrated that night, laughed harder, giggled with my friend's young children through dinner, and could not stop thinking about his words.

Several days later I headed back home feeling quite rosy about my existence.

I would like to write that the experience changed me dramatically and I became a caring physician who discovered a newfound love for his patients and his work.

And that transformation happened, sort of... for a short while...kind of...

HEROIC RETURN FROM TELLURIDE

I'M DEPUTIZED AND FINALLY PLAY DOCTOR

On the first day back from my life-affirming transformation in Telluride, I injected my newly discovered enthusiasm into clinic work: I was alive and healthy. Life was great. I handled patient's illnesses and concerns with confidence; dare I say, aplomb. Nothing would break my spirit.

Respiratory infections, colds, fussy infants—no problem, I enjoyed treating them all. I found myself excited to treat some challenging cases, and in walked a woman who was nauseated and vomiting.

Fantastic, thank you!

I quickly diagnosed her with pyelonephritis (a kidney infection) along with moderate dehydration.

Child's play.

I ordered an IV for rehydration, ran antibiotics through the same IV to get them into her body faster, and finished with an order for some anti-nausea medicine. She would be feeling better soon, and I felt all the better for being part of her recovery.

Next case, please!

A possible case of pneumonia? I ordered a chest X-ray.

Next case! Come on, challenge me!

Ah, a little guy with a laceration across his face—love it! I could already visualize exactly how things would go: I'd gently reassure the parents that I could do an excellent job; however, I would also give them the option of driving to the children's hospital where their injured little skateboarding brigand could be sewn up under the haze of really good drugs that I couldn't offer here.

They would want to stay in this clinic with the obviously confident doctor who'd been honest about the options for their son's care. I would relax the kid with my own calm demeanor and talk with him as I would to an adult. I would then sit down to perform some plastic surgery.

Didn't I say challenge me?

Everything went exactly as I had imagined. As I cleaned the skin around the boy's wound, I began wondering when I would hear what the chest X-Ray looked like on the poor patient with possible pneumonia or pulmonary poppycock; or if a nurse would ask if she should start a second bag of IV fluids for the woman with the kidney infection.

Then I would answer with self-assured poise, *"Let's give her a second bag of NS."* It would sound official, and the parents of the bleeding boy would be impressed that their child was in the hands of a professional—albeit a slightly over-caffeinated, high on life, fast-speaking version of a doctor only months out of medical school—but a professional physician, nonetheless.

And I was just kidding on the pulmonary poppycock comment, but the alliteration fit with my as-yet-undisturbed joyous and poetically redemptive return to medicine.

The curtains surrounding the suture room opened and I looked up, ready to give a Chuck Yeager-style cool and calm response to the nurse asking about IVs and X-rays. But instead of the nurse tossing me a medical patient question I could easily answer, there stood our receptionist staring at me with a look conveying trouble. I raised a questioning eyebrow, wondering what she wanted, as I was about to start a very important procedure.

"There's a lady up front who needs to talk with you."

What could possibly be more important than my playing doctor?

Jokingly I asked, "Why? Is she upset with me?"

"No, with me," the receptionist replied.

I peeled off my sterile gloves and walked out. On the way to the front room the receptionist pulled me aside, likely to confess her unbridled appreciation of my medical skills.

Instead, she warned me that the woman outside was *really* pissed-off because we weren't taking care of the patient she'd brought with her, even though the receptionist had already offered to take him back to an exam room while the woman checked him in.

And there it was, reality crashing down on my fleeting moment of medical happiness—one statement, by one pissy and outraged family member, to snap me out of my fantasy world.

My transformed attitude about medicine was about to end less than two hours into its very existence.

I walked into the reception area and was confronted by a 4'2" banshee. I'd never actually seen a banshee but was convinced I was now meeting one: a mean little shrew beast who'd never had good sex, and was angry at men, the world, and specifically everyone in my clinic—possibly including herself.

But I smiled and asked how I could help?

"Is this urgent care?" She replied. "It says urgent care, and I have a sick man here." She pointed to a man sitting calmly in a chair smiling back at me. "He is very sick! And nobody is taking care of him."

"Why don't we take him back to an exam room while you check him in?" I tried to politely interject.

"He's very sick and you're doing nothing for him. I am reporting this to the board of medicine. I am a physician. This is a disgrace." And now she started shouting, "He is sitting here, dehydrated, and you're doing nothing. I'll have this place shut down! You dare call it urgent care?!"

Of course I'm not taking care of him because I'm being yelled at by you, while I have other patients waiting for me to complete their care.

I was suddenly not enjoying the moment. Patients in the waiting room watched me try to employ my now futilely lost Chuck Yeager calmness in battle. I just stared at her for almost twenty seconds, bewildered.

I was shocked. I'd never dealt with anyone like this in the clinic and wished she would just go away. I tried another rational line.

"Look, I have other patients back there who are also sick, and we will get your husband back there as soon as possible, now--"

"That's my *dad*!"

My comment did nothing to mollify the situation.

"What do you have back there?" she continued. "Oh, what, a cut? Some X-rays? An IV? That can wait. You're pathetic. I'm reporting you as well. They're taking your license away."

I stood silently amazed that she somehow knew exactly what was going on back in the treatment rooms.

I was also wondering if she was actually some board member of a physician group that was going to take my license away—which put me in an embarrassing situation with all the other patients watching.

Finally one of those waiting room patients stood up to help me calm this nightmare into somebody rational. He was a really big-guy, around 6'4", who obviously spent lots of free time lifting weights in front of mirrors because he looked like a pale chiseled version of the Hulk.

He walked over to the mean little woman saying, "Lady, why don't you check your dad in and let the doctor get back to the other patients--"

His Good Samaritan efforts were cut short as Medusa in her miniature modern form spun round and started swinging at him with her little balled-up fists, screeching, *"Do you have an 84-year-old sick man with you?"* And she continued pounding him in the chest like a mean little weasel boxing an elephant.

I was now in complete shock. The situation had spiraled totally out of control, and I needed to do something to break up this episode of Jerry Springer-visits-my-strip-mall.

I ran around the desk proclaiming, "OK, enough, this is not happening in my clinic, no more!" I separated the huffing banshee from the big guy who was unscathed from her blows. Finally I had exerted my authority.

But before I could say anything else, the wife of the intervening pale hulk stood up and announced that both she and her husband were in police enforcement, and she wanted me to call 911 and charge the shrew witch with assault.

Seriously? I took a deep breath, thought about it, and I had to agree that technically the wee beast had assaulted her husband, and that she had a right to call 911—although nobody had been hurt, and I just wanted to go back to my safe play world of being the doctor.

I dialed 911 and handed the law enforcement wife the phone while I tried to calm the angry lady one last time, "Look, we can handle taking care of your husband, *sorry!* Your dad, right here. We do that all the time. But if you want, we can call an ambulance and have him taken to the ER so that he gets care at an ER. It will probably be a four-hour wait longer than here, but you can do that, gladly."

At this point my attempt to handle the situation was superseded by the father of the little guy with the cut on his head.

He calmly strode over to the woman and knelt by her side (He even wore a leather jacket which made him look more like Chuck Yeager than me), and began kindly empathizing with her situation, "It must be pretty stressful having a sick dad."

232

She then opened her heart to him, divulging how she'd been really stressed, and that on the drive over to the clinic, a big rig eighteen-wheeler truck had hit her car and driven off, and they were both injured. Now we all started to feel like uncompassionate cads.

Then the woman on the phone announced that the police were on their way over—at which point the evil witch of the west jumped up and announced she was leaving.

However, standing at the front door, barring her escape was the burly guy with his arm crossed, "No way lady!" He looked around at us all and declared, "I'm making a citizen's arrest!"

Things were now officially freaking bananas.

What the hell was a citizen's arrest?

Was I supposed to stick her in a cell in the back and stand guard with a handmade sheriff's badge?

But before I actually figured out where I could find supplies to craft a badge to wear, the police showed up and informed me that the mean-spirited woman had actually hit the truck on the way over. And it was she who had jumped out of her car and *assaulted* the truck driver before *she* drove off and arrived here to ruin my day.

They'd been searching for her ever since. The truck guy was not pressing charges, so they just needed to resolve this latest situation.

While the police escorted her outside, I went to check on her father. He turned out to be hypoxic (very low on oxygen) due to pneumonia that I could hear rattling in his lungs. And then he started vomiting. I needed an ambulance to take him to the hospital because his oxygen levels were dangerously low.

I walked outside, the day's earlier enthusiasm in shambles, to tell the woman how her father was doing.

To no surprise of mine, the police were wasting their breath trying to out-shout the woman to please shut-up as she hollered that she was in law enforcement and that they were all going to be arrested.

I interrupted their otherwise unpleasant conversation to relay the need to send her father to the hospital by ambulance.

She immediately cursed me with several colorful sentences regarding me losing my license. Oh yes, I was feeling really warm and fuzzy about the joys of medicine right now.

LATER THAT NIGHT, AFTER FINALLY SEWING UP THE YOUNG BOY'S face, treating the cases of pneumonias and pyelonephritis, and seeing a continuous stream of patients, I was exhausted.

I walked into a room to treat a woman for *excruciating* pain. She had been in hysterics ever since entering the clinic. It had already taken several minutes of swimming through her drama for the nurses to uncover that she was here because her knees hurt and that she expected Workman's Compensation to pay for her injury.

When I entered the exam room, she was lying on her side bawling in pain. Apparently my newly-fired compassion had been quelled in one short day as I ignored her tears and asked how she'd hurt her knees without even offering a tissue. I expected a story involving some falling, twisting, or banging. But it turned out that her "injury" had been sustained when she stood up from her chair at work and had experienced knee pain.

I had no idea why Workman's Compensation was paying for her sore knees, but I calmed her down and reassured her that we would help figure out the source of her pain.

As I left the room to order an X-ray to help evaluate her for likely osteoarthritis (wear and tear of her cartilage), she flopped over and wailed, "What about my emotional instability?"

"*What?*"

"What are you going to do for my emotional instability?"

"Nothing, you're here because your knees hurt."

At which point she burst back into tears. The X-rays were completely normal. Her knee exam was normal. Her DOPL report on the other hand, displayed a respectable history of narcotic abuse. When I declined prescribing her any narcotics, she left the clinic cursing my lack of compassion.

I was *really* enjoying my return to medicine.

A brief addendum: The same patient returned weeks later, apologized to me for her unkind words, thanked me for being up front about her addiction, then asked for a prescription for pain medicine for a headache. *Denied.*

And then, even later that same night, minutes before the clinic finally closed its doors on a day of mayhem, a rush of people showed up. I was now, thanks to their tardy decisions to seek medical help until right before we closed, going to stay and see patients until well after midnight.

Finally, closer to 1 a.m., I went to see the last patient, a young woman with a headache. Most people we encountered with headaches wanted narcotics and at this late hour, with a mountain of patient's charts waiting for me to complete, I would probably just give her a prescription for a few pills of pain medicine and tell her to go to the ER if it persisted. But first I had to make sure I wasn't missing anything more serious, like meningitis or a bleed inside her head.

My first question was, "So, you're here for a headache?"

To which she replied, "Well, uh...I guess so."

At one in the morning, after I'd been seeing patients for seventeen hours, if the patient didn't know why they were there, I thought we should all go home, get some rest, and attack that tricky question in the morning. But she finally agreed that she was there for a headache.

I went through my list of headache questions, almost all of which were yes or no type queries—and these cagey inquiries almost fried her precious few working neurons.

"Have you had headaches like this before?" I asked.

"I don't know. Maybe?" she replied.

What was I supposed to do if she didn't know the answers? Make them up myself?

Finally she told me she had "bumps" on her head that felt heavy. I felt her head and found no such bumps.

"The bumps are giving me terrible headaches today. My head hurts, why does my head hurt?"

"I don't know," I replied and began to wonder if there was something really wrong with her, like a stroke, too much radiation, or a drug overdose.

"Is it the bumps?" she asked again.

"I don't feel any bumps," I told her and then turned to her accompanying friend and asked, "Is she acting normal to you?" I was concerned that there was something abnormal going on and needed her objective third party thoughts on her friend's apparent confusion.

"Oh yes, she's totally fine, just the headache," her friend replied.

"Is it because I think too much?" the patient asked. *"Do I think too much?"*

I paused, trying not to laugh, "Doubtfully."

"I think too much," she insisted.

"No, no, I really don't think that's it," I replied again. "But then again, who knows."

I examined her and everything was completely normal. She seemed overwhelmingly thrilled that I wrote her a prescription for ibuprofen, all the while being shocked that I couldn't feel bumps on her head. She left the clinic insisting that her headache was the result of her thinking too much.

I sat alone at my desk finishing the day's charts and started thinking about my paltry existence in the world of strip mall medicine, struggling to give the best care to these patients. And how was I going to become an actor? Then there was my self-imposed messy personal life.

I had started spending some time with the stunning woman who had sat next to me at the yoga workshop. Turns out we had many similar interests, enjoyed playing in the mountains. She had a fantastic sense of humor. Even our dogs were the same age and got along great. But typical of me, I made things complicated as I was still harboring feelings for the woman who had broken up with me several months prior.

What was I doing with my life? I began to get a headache. Maybe that last patient was right all along? Maybe thinking too much caused headaches? Or perhaps a seventeen-hour shift without time to drink water or go to the bathroom was the cause?

But I decided to try and stop overthinking everything as it was fatiguing and didn't seem to help anything. And guess what? It didn't help my personal life at all. But the patient care became easier. I constantly wrestled with the care of every patient. I decided to try adding some confidence into my decision making without second guessing everything—and I felt more relaxed (slightly)—although I still wore myself out with tough cases, researching the case more than I needed, and seeking consults where I know other doctors would just send the patient away with a referral to see a specialist.

———

A FEW NIGHTS LATER, HAVING WORKED A FOURTEEN-HOUR DAY, I SAT talking with my last patient, an eleven-year-old boy with diarrhea. I went through my rote list of questions for patients with diarrhea. What a perfect way to end the day.

Suddenly his three-year-old sister asked their mom, "Why is the doctor asking gross questions?"

In my tired state, I burst out laughing, "That's the funniest thing I've heard all day," I told her. She just giggled.

Two days later the mom walked in with the same three-year-old girl, who had stuck beads up both nostrils. I told the mother that in most cases, with slippery beads up the nose of somebody her age, I would likely have to send them to the children's hospital. I'd been unsuccessful in removing objects from kids' noses on so many occasions that I'd stopped traumatizing the youngsters with my attempts at sticking curettes deep inside their heads.

The little girl, obviously terrified by the prospect of a doctor removing the beads, was already pretty jumpy—the exact type of patient who would squirm and scream the second I came near her nose with a medical instrument. The mother understood she would probably need to go to the children's ER, and everybody relaxed.

The nurse had been chatting with the patient while I spoke with the mother and discovered that the little girl had a small crush on an imaginary boy, which she was joking about and making the girl laugh—which gave me an idea. I reminded the girl how she'd made me laugh the other night when I was asking gross questions. She giggled and I wondered if she could make me laugh again by blowing her nose for me.

She refused, stating she didn't know how. When I asked her to try, she only inhaled the beads deeper. I joked some more and stepped outside the room, challenging her to blow her nose hard enough for me to hear her.

And she did.

We kept playing games, giggling about being able to blow snot and boogers out her nose, and how gross that was. She started laughing and blowing her nose, trying to gross me out, and much to everyone's amazement, eventually shot a shiny bead out each nostril.

The patient left and I realized I must have learned something: I could finally get foreign bodies out of a kid's nose.

The nurse turned to me, "*See*, all that acting pays off."

I finally had my big role, playing doctor.

As for the stunning woman who unrolled her mat next to mine at the yoga workshop? Well, she was extremely patient with me (an understatement), and we're still together all these years later.

MYSELF, EVER I BE, ALWAYS YOURS, DR. JOHNNY UTAH.

ACKNOWLEDGEMENTS

My wife's love and support is amazing. She recognizes my stubbornness, smiles at my bumbling ways, and allows both to flourish while managing a fluctuating household menagerie of kids, friends and animals. None of us work well without her.

I am so thankful for my three wonderful kids whose love and celebratory spirit keeps me buoyed through the intrinsic self-questioning of putting out these books.

To my mother, her repeated read throughs saved these books from being grammatical nightmares.

To my friends who believed in my crazy ideas to write, to act, to become a doctor.

Hoke, my guru for living well and remembering life's priorities.

Chris, for keeping me accountable, continually inspired, and willing to laugh at ourselves.

Brad, keeping me alive and healthy, and continually demonstrating that there is one acceptable way to practice medicine, the right way.

Thank you to all the patients over the many years who trusted me with your wellbeing and health.

Thank you to all the teachers, doctors, and staff, that have patiently instructed me over the years.

These books are so much better thanks to my wonderful

editor, Anne Cole Norman. Thank you for your hard work and encouragement.

The cover designs, which always make me laugh, are due to the wonderful creative talents of Caroline Johnson. Thank you for work and amazing patience.

The marketing and planning are thanks to the lovely and brilliant Louise Newland. Thank you for your tireless support of me and the books.

For Valter, who opens his arms to the world to share his enthusiasm for life.

ABOUT THE AUTHOR

John loves his family, his friends, skiing, biking, running, cooking, traveling, writing and watching films. John received his M.D. at the University of Utah, which is where he also completed his residency training. He received a B.A. from Georgetown University—where he did not take a single pre-med class.

John has been a river rafting guide, ski race coach, assistant soccer coach, bagel baker, environmental entrepreneur, screenwriter, film director, and expedition doctor.

He attempts to stay healthy, but still falls off his bike (a lot). Fortunately, his wife and kids are there to pick him up.